POLLY TEALE

Polly Teale is the Joint Artistic Director of Shared Experience
Theatre Company. *Jane Eyre* is the first of three plays exploring
the work and world of the Brontë family. The other plays are *After
Mrs Rochester*, based on the life of Jean Rhys and her novel *Wide
Sargasso Sea* (itself inspired by *Jane Eyre*), and *Brontë*, evoking
the real and imagined world of the Brontës. All three plays are
published by Nick Hern Books.

In addition to directing the premiere productions of these three
plays for Shared Experience – and winning the Evening Standard
Best Director Award for *After Mrs Rochester* – Polly's work for
the company includes directing *The Clearing*, *A Doll's House*, *The
House of Bernarda Alba*, *Desire under the Elms*, *Madame Bovary:
Breakfast with Emma* and co-directing *War and Peace* and *The
Mill on the Floss* with Nancy Meckler.

Her other directing credits include *Angels and Saints* for Soho
Theatre; *The Glass Menagerie* at the Lyceum, Edinburgh; *Miss
Julie* at the Young Vic; *Babies* and *Uganda* at the Royal Court; *A
Taste of Honey* for English Touring Theatre; *Somewhere* at the
National Theatre; *Waiting at the Water's Edge* at The Bush
Theatre; *What Is Seized* at the Drill Hall; *Ladies in the Lift* at
Soho Poly; *Flying*, *Manpower* and *Other Voices* at the National
Theatre Studio.

Polly's writing credits also include *Afters* for BBC Screen Two
and *Fallen* for the Traverse Theatre, Edinburgh, and the Drill Hall,
London.

D0262861

Jane Eyre

adapted from Charlotte Brontë's novel by
POLLY TEALE
for Shared Experience

with Notes by Polly Teale

NICK HERN BOOKS
LONDON
www.nickhernbooks.co.uk

A Nick Hern Book

This adaptation of *Jane Eyre* first published in Great Britain
in 1998 as an original paperback by Nick Hern Books Limited,
14 Larden Road, London W3 7ST

Reprinted 2001
Reprinted with revisions 2006

Typeset by Country Setting, Kingsdown, Kent CT14 8ES
Printed and bound in Great Britain by Biddles, King's Lynn

A CIP catalogue record for this book is available from
the British Library

ISBN-13   978 1 85459 329 0
ISBN-10   1 85459 329 3

'I am afraid of nothing but myself.'

Charlotte Brontë

Brontë on Brontë

'I am a very coarse, commonplace wretch. I have some qualities which make me very miserable, some feelings . . . that very, very few people in the world can at all understand. I don't pride myself on these peculiarities, I strive to conceal and suppress them as much as I can, but they burst out sometimes and then those who see the explosion despise me, and I hate myself for days afterwards.'

'Throughout my early youth . . . I felt myself incapable of feeling and acting as most people felt and acted; . . . unintentionally, I showed everything that passed in my heart and sometimes storms were passing through it. In vain I tried to imitate . . . the serene and even temper of my companions . . . '

'I could not restrain the ebb and flow of blood in my arteries and that ebb and flow always showed itself in my face and in my hard and unattractive features. I wept in secret.'

'The human heart has hidden treasures
In secret kept, in silence sealed – '

from Evening Solace, 1846

On Adapting *Jane Eyre*

Returning to *Jane Eyre* fifteen years after I read it as a teenager
I found, not the horror story I remembered, but a psychological
drama of the most powerful kind. Everything and everyone in the
story is seen, larger than life, through the magnifying glass of
Jane's psyche. Why though, I asked myself, did she invent a
madwoman locked in an attic to torment her heroine? Why is Jane
Eyre, a supremely rational young woman, haunted by a vengeful
she-devil? Why do these two women exist in the same story?

I had forgotten that the novel began with another image of incar-
ceration: another female locked away for breaking the rules of
allowed behaviour. Jane Eyre is shut up in the Red Room when,
for the first time in her young life, she allows her temper to erupt,
losing control of herself in an attack of rage. Jane is told that God
will strike her dead 'in the midst of one of her tantrums.' She is
so terrified she loses consciousness. The message is clear. For a
Victorian woman to express her passionate nature is to invite the
severest of punishment. Jane must keep her fiery spirit locked
away if she is to survive. Could it be that Jane and the madwoman
are not in fact opposites. That like all the most frightening ghosts
Bertha Mason exists not in the real world but in Jane's imagination?

I have come to see the novel as a quest, a passionate enquiry.
How is it possible for Jane as a woman to be true to herself in
the world in which she lives? Each of the women in the novel
suggests a possible role: from the excessive artificiality of Blanche
Ingram to the silent stoicism of Helen Burns we see the range of
choices available. Jane, like Brontë, is 'poor, obscure and plain'
and yet hidden inside is a 'secret self'; the huge imagination
glimpsed in Jane's visionary paintings of foreign lands. Although
Brontë spent most of her life in a remote Yorkshire village she had
a great longing to overpass the horizon of her restricted existence.
It is significant that Bertha is a foreigner. She comes from the land
of Brontë's imagination, from a land of hot rain and hurricanes.
She is both dangerous and exciting. She is passionate and sexual.
She is angry and violent. She is the embodiment of everything that
Jane, a Victorian woman, must never be. She is perhaps everything
that Brontë feared in herself and longed to express.

Polly Teale, September 1997

Charlotte Brontë: a Passionate Woman

What kind of person was Charlotte Brontë? Formidably
intelligent, impatient, prone to deep depression, but above all
passionate. Her passionate spirit is evident in every aspect of her
life: in her literary ambition, her anger at perceived injustice, her
frustration with the limitations imposed upon one of her sex and
social position, and in her quest for love.

Her anger is evident within the first few chapters of *Jane Eyre* – at
the injustice of Jane's treatment at the hands of the Reed family,
and at Jane's experiences at Lowood School. The Lowood episode
is a fictionalised account of Charlotte's own childhood experience
at the Clergy Daughters' School at Cowan Bridge. The treatment
of Helen Burns and Jane at the hands of Mr Brocklehurst and
Miss Scatcherd is portrayed with such raw passion and burning
sense of injustice that it's impossible not to side entirely with the
girls, or to have any sympathy with their persecutors. We don't
have to look far to discover the motive for Charlotte's anger: she
lost her two elder sisters Maria and Elizabeth at Cowan Bridge
to tuberculosis, and blamed her own stunted growth on the
conditions there.

Charlotte felt the loss of Maria and Elizabeth acutely: from being
one of the younger sisters she had suddenly become the eldest,
and she often felt inadequate to the task. Later in life Charlotte
recalled Maria's mildness, wisdom and fortitude of character, and
she was to be the model for Helen Burns in *Jane Eyre*. Although
some readers have felt that the saintliness of her character
stretches the bounds of credibility, Charlotte insisted 'I have
exaggerated nothing there: I abstained from recording much that
I remember respecting her, lest the narrative should sound
incredible.'

After the horrors of Cowan Bridge, Charlotte's next experience
of school was far happier. She attended Roe Head School, about
twenty miles from her home at Haworth, between 1831 and 1832.
Charlotte met her two greatest friends at Roe Head, Ellen Nussey
and Mary Taylor. Mary gives us a glimpse of the fourteen-year-
old Charlotte's arrival at Roe Head: 'She looked a little old
woman, so short-sighted that she always appeared to be seeking
something . . . She was very shy and nervous, and spoke with a

strong Irish accent.' Although Charlotte had a difficult start at Roe
Head, with her oddities and appearance a source of amusement to
the other pupils, her qualities were quickly recognised. She had an
exceptionally powerful intellect and great curiosity. Ellen Nussey
recalled 'she picked up every scrap of information concerning
painting, sculpture, poetry, music, etc., as if it were gold'.

Her return to Roe Head in 1835 as a teacher was, however, a
miserable experience. She had little or no patience with her slower
pupils, and although her feelings had, of course, to be masked
from public view they are given full vent in her journal:

> . . . am I to spend all the best part of my life in this wretched
> bondage, forcibly suppressing my rage at the idleness, the
> apathy and the hyperbolical and asinine stupidity of these
> fat-headed oafs and on compulsion assuming an air of
> kindness, patience and assiduity?

This went to the heart of Charlotte's dilemma. Being the daughter
of a prominent clergyman conferred her with middle class status,
but the family had no money. For a woman of her generation
options were severely limited. Marriage was one, but with no
fortune, Charlotte had early accepted that there was little or
no prospect of that. The other was to work, but there were few
careers open to a woman beyond teaching and governessing.
What this passage demonstrates is that Charlotte understood that
she must quell her raging passions for the sake of social accept-
ability, but the strain of doing so was, for her, almost intolerable.
'If you knew my thoughts' she wrote to Ellen Nussey, 'the dreams
that absorb me; and the fiery imagination that at times eats me up
and makes me feel society as it is, wretchedly insipid, you would
pity and I dare say despise me'.

Charlotte was torn between the demands of duty, and the call of
her 'fiery imagination'. After her spell at Roe Head she took a
succession of posts as governess, none of which she had the
tenacity to hold down for very long. Eventually imagination
gained the upper hand when she gave rein to her literary ambition.

Charlotte's passionate imagination found its earliest expression
in games and stories which were inspired by a box of wooden
soldiers given to her brother Branwell by their father when
Charlotte was ten. She and Branwell invented the kingdom of
Angria, based on accounts of expeditions to Africa which they had
read in their father's journal. Written in tiny handwriting in small
books, these stories allowed Charlotte to explore a secret world of

exotic lands and titanic characters, but eventually she came to see the fictional limitations of Angria, and in a fragment dating from 1839 known as the 'Farewell to Angria' she records how she longs 'to quit for a while that burning clime where we have sojourned too long . . . and turn now to a cooler region, where the dawn breaks grey and sober'. But something of that fascination with distant foreign lands survives in *Jane Eyre*, where within the first couple of pages, Jane's youthful imagination is caught up in a book which describes 'the vast sweep of the Arctic Zone, and those forlorn regions of dreary space'. Later, of course, we will meet Bertha, Rochester's first wife, who comes from an utterly different place: the West Indies, with its oranges and pineapples, tropical flowers, warm sea, and violent summer storms.

Although Charlotte had no expectation of marriage she did in time receive a proposal – from the Reverend Henry Nussey, Ellen's brother. Charlotte was not his first choice, but since romantic love seemed not to enter into the equation for him it didn't much matter who the woman was. Although Charlotte could see clearly the advantages of marriage to Henry she turned him down decisively. 'I had not, and never could have, that intense attachment which would make me willing to die for him – and if ever I marry it must be in that light of adoration that I will regard my husband.' To Henry she wrote 'As for me you do not know me, I am not the serious, grave cool-headed individual you suppose – you would think me romantic and eccentric – you would say I was satirical and severe'.

It was in Brussels that Charlotte's passion was to be fully engaged by a man. In 1842 she received a letter from Mary Taylor who was finishing her education there. Mary urged Charlotte to join her. Charlotte's reaction on reading Mary's letter was intense: 'I hardly knew what swelled to my throat as I read her letter – such a vehement impatience of restraint and steady work, such a strong wish for wings... such an urgent thirst to see – to know to learn – something internal seemed to expand boldly for a minute. I was tantalised with the consciousness of faculties unexercised . . . '

The man who helped her 'to see to know to learn' was Monsieur Constantin Heger, professor of rhetoric at the Pensionnat Heger. At last she had found someone who recognised her literary talent and whose opinion carried all the weight of a fine intellect and informed judgement. She had searched before, sending Robert Southey, one of her idols, some of her poems at the end of 1836. There is a retrospective irony about the reply of the then Poet

Laureate, whose work is now mostly unread, to a woman whose novels have achieved enduring fame: 'Literature cannot be the business of a woman's life, and it ought not to be. The more she is engaged in her proper duties, the less leisure will she have for it, even as an accomplishment and a recreation'.

The passion she felt for M. Heger, a married man, was never to be consummated. There is no doubt that she was attracted to him, but the attraction was as much intellectual as it was emotional or physical. Like Rochester he was not handsome: indeed Charlotte once described him as 'a little black ugly being', but 'his mind was indeed my library, and whenever it was opened to me, I entered bliss'. Charlotte was distraught when, during her second year at the Pensionnat, Heger increasingly distanced himself from her, probably under the instruction of his wife who had become concerned about the relationship.

Charlotte finally managed to drag herself away from this unhealthy situation at the beginning of 1844. She wrote to Ellen Nussey: 'I suffered much before I left Brussels. I think, however long I live, I shall not forget what the parting with M. Heger cost me'. But in one of her last essays for her master she was able boldly, and rightly, to proclaim: 'My lord, I believe that I have talent . . . My lord, I believe that I have Genius.' As Lyndall Gordon has observed, ' . . . it was part of the cure of the Angrian drug for Charlotte to . . . experience genuine passion, genuine pain.' Her time at the Pensionnat Heger may have cost her dear, but what she gained intellectually and emotionally from the experience saved her eventually from the life of stagnation which she feared so much, and freed her to write the passionate, controlled, realistic and fully human novels for which she is famous.

Eventually, Charlotte was to marry – in 1854, to her father's curate, Arthur Bell Nicholls. The marriage took place in the face of Patrick Brontë's opposition and her own initial reluctance. But the marriage proved happy, if tragically brief. Charlotte died the following year, aged 39, carrying her unborn child.

Stuart Leeks

JANE EYRE

I am greatly indebted to Helen Edmundson
for her inspirational adaptations of
Anna Karenina, *The Mill on the Floss* and *War and Peace*,
which were the starting point and basis of this work.

Also to Nancy Meckler, Liz Ranken and all of
the original company whose input was invaluable.

Production Notes

Central to the adaptation is the idea that hidden inside the sensible, frozen Jane exists another self who is passionate and sensual.

Bertha (trapped in the attic) embodies the fire and longing which Jane must lock away in order to survive in Victorian England.

At the beginning of the story, Jane reads a book about foreign lands. Bertha plays out Jane's secret imaginings, conjuring up the pictures she sees in her head. Bertha becomes wild and abandoned as Jane allows her inner world to take over. This is only possible because Jane is alone and can let down her guard. When John Reed enters the room Jane struggles to control and conceal Bertha until the point where Bertha breaks free, springing forward and attacking John Reed. From this moment to the end of Scene One, where Jane forces Bertha back into the red room and locks her in, there is a struggle between the inner and the outer self for control. In leaving Bertha behind, Jane has chosen to lock away the side of herself which is unacceptable to others. From this point onwards Bertha can no longer speak. Although they are now separated, Bertha continues to express the feelings that Jane is trying to conceal. She does this through movement and sound. These movements should affect Jane's body as if Bertha were a force inside her. However, when she is with others she must endeavour to conceal these eruptions and maintain her outer poise. This results in a strained stiffness and tension which is the body trying to suppress its emotional life. When Jane is alone there are moments when she lets rip and Bertha's movements and hers are similarly extreme.

At the beginning of the play Bertha is dressed as a child in a shorter skirt, as is Jane. When we arrive at Thornfield Bertha has taken on the identity of Rochester's mad wife. She now wears a long skirt, ripped and burnt at the edges. Her face and body are dirty and bandaged. Her hair is a huge matted dreadlock. Her movements have become animal-like as are the sounds she makes. In the script there are indications as to the nature of Bertha's movements as they were in the original production. It is better however to use these as a guideline and invent your own. Ask yourself what emotion Jane is secretly feeling and allow Bertha to physicalise the essence of that feeling. Because she is 'mad', she should be uncensored and highly expressive. There should be a strong sexual element to her movements. Although she has the capacity to be violent she is also capable of tenderness. The attic room is very dimly lit whenever we see Bertha during another scene. Her presence should heighten the emotional energy, not distract. We found that any violent or sudden movement from Bertha had to correspond with an eruption of movement and feeling in Jane.

The Design

The design requires a raised level to represent the red room and attic. Although the room must have a door which can be locked, it is not necessary to have walls or other naturalistic details, apart from possibly a chair. The different settings of the scenes are created with a minimum of furniture and props. All food, drink and water is invisible. All scene changes are done by the company. The original production had a live cello played by the actor who played Mason and the teacher at Lowood.

Jane Eyre was first performed by Shared Experience Theatre
Company at the Wolsey Theatre Ipswich on 4 September 1997 and
subsequently at the Cambridge Arts Theatre, Oxford Playhouse,
Poole Arts Centre, the Young Vic Theatre, London, Warwick Arts
Centre, Richmond Theatre and Chichester Festival Theatre. The
parts were played by members of the company as follows

MRS REED and MRS FAIRFAX	Joan Blackham
BROCKLEHURST, PILOT THE DOG, LORD INGRAM and ST JOHN RIVERS	Antony Byrne
ROCHESTER and JOHN REED	James Clyde
JANE EYRE	Monica Dolan
BESSIE, BLANCHE INGRAM, GRACE POOLE, DIANA RIVERS, WOMAN	Hannah Miles
BERTHA	Pooky Quesnel
RICHARD MASON and CELLIST	Philip Rham
ABIGAIL, HELEN BURNS, ADELE, and MARY RIVERS	Octavia Walters

All other characters played by members of the company

Adapted and directed by Polly Teale
Company Movement Liz Ranken
Designer Neil Warmington
Lighting designer Chris Davey
Composer Peter Salem
Production Manager Alison Ritchie
Company Stage Manager Sid Charlton
Deputy Stage Manager James Byron
ASM/Props Paul Williams
Sound Operator Julie Winkles
Costume Supervisor Yvonne Milnes
Script Advisors Debbie Isitt, Nancy Meckler

Characters

JANE

BERTHA

Suggested doubling for other characters

ROCHESTER
JOHN REED

MRS REED
MRS FAIRFAX

BESSIE
BLANCHE
GRACE POOLE
DIANA RIVERS
WOMAN

ABIGAIL
HELEN
ADELE
GIRL IN MARKET
MARY RIVERS

BROCKLEHURST
PILOT, *Rochester's dog*
LORD INGRAM
FOOTMAN
CLERGYMAN
SAINT JOHN RIVERS

MUSICIAN
TEACHER
ROCHESTER'S HORSE
RICHARD MASON

MEN IN WEST INDIES, MARKET SELLERS and
SCHOOLGIRLS are played by members of the company

Scene 1

JANE *is holding a large book. She stares at it with excitement but doesn't dare to open it. BERTHA, who is hidden behind her, reaches out and opens the first page. JANE reads aloud to BERTHA. BERTHA listens and enacts, conjuring up the scene as JANE describes it. BERTHA makes the sound of cawing birds and arctic winds. Their limbs are entangled as if they are one person.*

JANE. The vast sweep of the Arctic zone lies buried under frost and snow. These forsaken regions of dreary space are seldom seen by human eyes. The extreme cold and biting wind make *(She hesitates over the word.)* uninhabitable this frozen waste.

  JANE *shivers.* BERTHA *takes the book and turns to her favourite page.*

BERTHA. The tropical clime of the West Indies has been described as a paradise on earth.

JANE. The sunshine and heavy rainfall give rise to abundant growth.

  BERTHA *plucks an imaginary fruit from the air and feeds it to* JANE.

  Oranges and pineapples grow on the trees. Huge tropical flowers scent the air. The sea is warm as a bath and the light is golden day in, day out.

  BERTHA *rolls in the warm water. The movement is deeply sensual.* JANE *looks on excited but nervous, like someone indulging in forbidden pleasure.* BERTHA *begins to hum the rain dance song.* JANE *cannot resist reading on.*

  In the dry months of the winter the women dance and sing to bring the rains.

  BERTHA *springs to her feet.*

BERTHA. Let me see the picture.

  JANE *shows* BERTHA *a picture of a naked woman dancing. They squeal with excitement.* JANE *hides the book behind her back.* BERTHA *stands, her palms turned to the sky and head thrown back. She laughs and begins to dance.* JANE *watches her with delight and sways slightly in time.* BERTHA *sings as she dances. The dance becomes wilder and wilder.*

JANE. When the storm finally breaks it rains so hard there are rivers in the streets and through the houses.

BERTHA dances more wildly as if being drenched by the rain. She spins and laughs, her mouth wide open. She lets out a wild cry.

In Summer the hurricanes come. These 150 mile per hour winds can uproot trees and smash through houses. Tidal waves fifty feet high crash against the coastline causing havoc.

BERTHA has become the hurricane and then the tidal wave.

Every year several feet of the island disappear into the sea.

The game has become more and more abandoned as BERTHA *whips* JANE *into a frenzy of excitement. Suddenly footsteps are heard.* JANE *and* BERTHA *hide behind a chair. A boy,* JOHN REED *enters the room. He is carrying a catapult and looking for* JANE *who he does not see.*

JOHN. Madame Mope. Where is she?

BERTHA and JANE sit hidden beneath the chair.

JOHN. Tell Mama she is run out into the rain. Bad animal.

He tests his catapult and then looking down sees JANE's *foot sticking out from underneath the chair. He pushes the chair away, revealing* JANE *and* BERTHA *in a heap.*

JANE. What do you want?

JOHN. What do you want *Master Reed.*

He seats himself in the chair and points to the ground in front of him.

JOHN. I want you to come here.

JANE *comes to him as ordered. She is frightened and obedient.* BERTHA *follows reluctantly, staring at him with hatred.* JANE *struggles to conceal her.* JOHN *addresses* JANE *as if* BERTHA *were invisible.*

JOHN. What were you doing behind the chair?

JANE. I was reading.

JOHN. You were hiding. Sneaking around as usual. You have no business to take our books. You are a dependent as Mama's told you. You have no money. Your father left you none. You ought to beg – not live here with a gentleman's family like us and eat the same food as we do and wear clothes at Mama's expense. Mama says you are so plain it is not worth buying you pretty dresses. She says you are the plainest little girl she ever saw.

BERTHA *is beginning to snarl and stamp.* JANE *tries to conceal her.*

JOHN *gives* JANE *a backward push.*

JOHN. Get away from me.

BERTHA. Now.

JANE. I can't.

BERTHA. Tell him.

JANE. Can't.

JOHN. Go and stand by the door, away from the mirror and windows.

BERTHA. Don't move.

JANE. I've got to.

BERTHA. No.

JANE *does as told.* BERTHA *is dragged behind her.* JOHN *lifts the book that* JANE *was reading and goes as if to throw it at her. He laughs when she flinches and then taunts her again by pretending to throw the book a second time.* BERTHA *spits and snarls while* JANE, *terrified, tries to keep her hidden from view.* JOHN REED *roars with laughter at this picture of rage and terror.*

JOHN. Coward.

He goes to throw the book a third time. This time it is for real. Before the book leaves his hand BERTHA *has sprung forth wrestling it from him.* JANE *runs towards him.*

JANE. Wicked, cruel boy. You are like a slave driver.

BERTHA. A murderer . . . a monster.

JOHN. What! Did she say that to me?

BESSIE, *a servant has come to the door.*

JOHN. Wait till I tell Mama.

JANE *and* BERTHA *lunge at* JOHN, *biting his shoulder in a fit of violent rage.*

JOHN. Rat! Rat!

JANE *and* BERTHA *are dragged off by two servants,* BESSIE *and* ABIGAIL. MRS REED *appears at the door.*

BESSIE. What a fury to fly at Master John.

ABIGAIL. Did anyone ever see such a picture of passion?

MRS REED. Take her away to the red room and lock her in there.

JANE *and* BERTHA *are dragged through the house, fighting all the way.* MRS REED *embraces her son. It is apparent that* BERTHA *has bitten his shoulder and drawn blood.*

JANE *and* BERTHA *are thrust through a door into the red room.*

ABIGAIL. Hold her arms. She's like a mad cat.

BESSIE. For shame. For shame.

The servants try to force JANE *and* BERTHA *into a chair. They struggle.*

ABIGAIL. If you don't sit still you must be tied down. Bessie take off your garters.

JANE. No. Don't take them off. I will not stir.

JANE *tries to sedate* BERTHA *sitting on her and trying to cover her mouth.*

ABIGAIL. What shocking conduct Miss Eyre. To strike your master. She has torn his shirt with her biting.

BERTHA. How is he my master? Am I a servant?

JANE *stifles her.*

BESSIE. You ought to be aware, miss, that you are indebted to Mrs Reed. She keeps you. If she were to turn you off you'd have to go to the poorhouse. You should try to be useful and pleasant. If you are passionate and rude missis will send you away.

BESSIE *and* ABIGAIL *watch suspiciously.* JANE *has gained control and has her hand smothering* BERTHA's *mouth. She is still.*

BESSIE. She never did so before. She is usually so quiet. Too quiet almost for a child.

ABIGAIL. It was always in her. She's an underhand thing. I never saw a girl of her age with so much cover. Come, Bessie. We'll leave her.

BESSIE and ABIGAIL *leave shutting the door and locking it. JANE loosens her hold on* BERTHA *who immediately gets to her feet.*

BERTHA. Unjust. Unjust.

JANE. Why can I never please?

BERTHA. He is cruel and wicked.

JANE. Why is it useless to try and win anyone's favour?

BERTHA. He should be punished not me. He drowned a kitten in the stream. He set the dogs at the sheep. He snaps the heads off the flowers in the hothouse and laughs.

JANE. I dare commit no fault. I strive to fulfil every duty and I am called naughty and sullen and sneaking and . . .

BERTHA. Unjust. Unjust.

JANE. I will run away. I will not eat or drink. I will let myself die.

BERTHA. If Mr Reed had been alive he would have treated me kindly.

JANE. Ssh. Ssh. Ssh.

She tries to stifle BERTHA.

BERTHA. I have read that dead men can come back. They come back to punish the living who have failed to do their bidding as Mrs Reed has. She promised him to look after me and treat me as her own. He will come back and torment her.

JANE. Shut up. Shut up. He died in this room. He was laid out on that bed.

Silence. They stare out into the room. They are both afraid. BERTHA *goes to the door and tries the handle.* JANE *runs to the door and tries it also. The door is locked.* JANE *looks back into the room, so does* BERTHA.

BERTHA. Something moved. I saw something.

JANE *lets out a terrible scream.* BERTHA *pummels the door.* JANE *rattles the handle. The door opens. It is* BESSIE.

JANE. Let me out. Let me go.

She grabs BESSIE's *arm.*

JANE. There was somebody there.

MRS REED *appears in the doorway.*

MRS REED. What is all this? I gave orders that she should be left
until I came to her myself.

BESSIE. She screamed so loud ma'am.

MRS REED. She has screamed on purpose, as if she was in great
pain, but she only wanted to bring us all here. Let her go.
Loose her hand child.

JANE *lets go reluctantly.*

MRS REED. You cannot succeed in getting out by this trickery. I
had meant to free you shortly, but you will now stay here an
hour longer.

JANE. Aunt, have pity. Forgive me. I cannot endure it. I shall be
killed if . . .

MRS REED. You shall not be killed Jane Eyre. It is a sin to be
deceitful and lie. You must learn . . .

BERTHA *and* JANE (*together*). I am not a liar. If I were I should
say I loved you, but I don't love you. I dislike you the worst of
anybody in the world, except your son.

MRS REED (*coldly*). What more have you to say?

BERTHA *and* JANE (*together*). I am glad you are no relation of
mine. I will never call you aunt as long as I live. I will never
come to see you when I am grown and I will tell anyone who
asks me how you locked me up and treated me with cruelty.

MRS REED. How dare you affirm that, Jane Eyre?

BERTHA *and* JANE. How dare I? How dare I? Because it is the
truth.

You think I have no feelings, that I can do without one bit of
love or kindness, but I cannot live so. No one could live so . . .

MRS REED. She shall remain in here one hour longer. But it's
only on condition of perfect stillness and submission that I will
release her then. Henceforth my own children will play in the
drawing room. She will be confined to the nursery. I do not
choose that either John or his sisters should associate with her.

She turns and exits. BESSIE *follows locking the door behind her.*

BERTHA *runs to the door and shouts.*

BERTHA. They are not fit to associate with me.

BERTHA *is exhilarated. Breathless.* JANE *is mortified. Close to tears.*

JANE. How could you say such things?

BERTHA. It's true.

JANE. Look what you've done.

BERTHA. If good people are always obedient wicked people will have it all their own way . . . .

JANE. You have made them all hate me.

BERTHA. They will never be afraid and never change. They will get worse and worse . . .

JANE. No one will speak to me. I will be punished and punished.

BERTHA. When we are struck unfairly we must strike back. Very hard. To teach them never to do it again.

JANE *springs upon* BERTHA, *smothering her mouth.* BERTHA *lets out muffled cries .*

JANE. Shut up. Shut up. Shut up. Shut up.

BERTHA *struggles but* JANE *holds fast.* BERTHA *becomes gradually weakened and then finally flops in* JANE's *arms. She is still.* JANE *stares at* BERTHA, *horrified and then backs away. She runs at the door, flinging herself against it again and again. She faints. We hear the sound of feet. The door opens. It is* BESSIE. *She sees* JANE *lying on the floor. She rushes towards her. She sits* JANE *up.* BERTHA *stirs.* BESSIE *helps* JANE *to her feet.* BERTHA *sits up.* JANE *is helped towards the door as* BERTHA *crawls along the ground.* JANE *looks back and sees her following.* JANE *and* BESSIE *pass through the door.* BERTHA *grabs the handle, pulling it towards her.* JANE *grabs the handle on the other side. They wrestle in slow motion but* JANE *finally wins, pulling the door shut. We hear the key turn in the lock.* BERTHA *pummels the door, exhausted.*

Scene 2

Throughout this scene we can see BERTHA *still locked in the red room. She is restless and uneasy. When* JANE *is accused of being deceitful she rattles the door handle trying to get out. She expresses the anger which* JANE *herself cannot.* MRS REED *and* MR BROCKLEHURST *are looking at* JANE *who stares straight ahead.*

MRS REED. This is the little girl respecting whom I applied to you.

BROCKLEHURST. Her size is small. What is her age?

MRS REED. Ten years.

BROCKLEHURST. So much! . . . Your name, little girl?

JANE. Jane Eyre, sir.

BROCKLEHURST. Well, Jane. Are you a good girl?

There is silence. JANE *stares straight ahead aware of* MRS REED's *critical gaze.*

MRS REED. Perhaps the less said on that subject the better, Mr Brocklehurst.

BROCKLEHURST. No sight so sad as that of a naughty child. Do you know, Jane, where the wicked go after death?

JANE. They go to hell.

BROCKLEHURST. And what is hell?

JANE. A pit full of fire.

BROCKLEHURST. Bring me that candle.

JANE brings BROCKLEHURST *a burning candle and hands it to him.*

Now, Jane. Place your finger into the flame.

JANE. I cannot.

BROCKLEHURST. You cannot? You cannot put your finger into the flame and yet you would spend eternity burning in the fiery lake of sulphur. Tormented day and night, forever and ever.

JANE. No, sir.

BROCKLEHURST. Then what must you do to avoid it?

Pause.

JANE. I must keep in good health and not die.

BROCKLEHURST. But how is it possible when children younger than you are dying every day? Do you say your prayers night and day?

JANE. Yes sir.

BROCKLEHURST. Do you read your Bible?

JANE. Sometimes.

BROCKLEHURST. Only sometimes?

JANE. I like Revelations and the Book of Daniel and Genesis and a little bit of Exodus and some parts of Kings and Chronicles and Job and Jonah and . . .

BROCKLEHUST. And the Psalms. I hope you like them.

JANE. No, sir.

BROCKLEHURST. No?

JANE. Psalms are not interesting.

MRS REED. Mr Brocklehurst, as you see for yourself this girl has not quite the character and disposition I would wish for. I should be glad if the teachers at Lowood were requested to keep a strict eye on her and to guard, particularly against her worst fault, a tendency to deceit. As for the vacations, she will, with your permission, spend them always at school.

BROCKLEHURST. She shall be watched Mrs Reed. Little girl, come here. Read this book with prayer.

He hands her a pamphlet.

It tells of the awfully sudden death of a naughty girl not much older than yourself. A girl who thought it funny to shout out of her bedroom window onto the street 'Fire. Fire.' Of course, people came running with buckets full of water and ladders and ropes, only to find that there was no fire. Then one day, that naughtly little girl was alone in the house, when she smelt smoke. She opened the door onto the landing and the flames leapt towards her. She ran to the window and what did she shout?

Those same words. 'Fire. Fire' And did they believe her? They did not. They called her a liar.

During BROCKLEHURST's *story the sound of* BERTHA *trying to escape has been growing louder. As* BROCKLEHURST *and* MRS REED *exit,* JANE *begins to run as if she were*

running for her life. BERTHA *pounds the door.* JANE *has
run out into the garden, as far away from the house as she can
get. She tears the pamphlet to pieces and falls to the ground
and weeps.* BERTHA *too slumps exhausted. A distant voice
is heard. It is* BESSIE *calling her in to tea.* JANE *sits still
and does not answer.* BESSIE *appears, out of breath. She is
furious.*

BESSIE. Miss Jane. Where are you? (*She sees* JANE.) You
naughty thing. Why don't you come when you're called?

JANE. Come, Bessie. Don't scold. I shall be going away soon.

BESSIE. Gone away?

JANE. To school.

BESSIE (*surprised at* JANE's *answer*). And will you miss Bessie
when you're gone?

JANE. What does Bessie care for me? She's always scolding me.

BESSIE. Because you're such a queer, frightened shy little thing.
You should be more bold.

JANE. What? To get more knocks?

BESSIE. It's the way you start when I speak to you. It's so
provoking.

JANE. I don't think I'll ever be afraid of you again Bessie because
I've got used to you. Now I've a new set of people to dread.

BESSIE. If you dread them they'll dislike you.

JANE. As you do Bessie.

BESSIE. You sharp little thing. Listen the way she speaks.

JANE. You see!

BESSIE. Very well. Tomorrow afternoon Mrs Reed and the
children are not at home. I shall ask Cook to bake us a cake
and you and I will have tea together. You shall have the special
plate with the bird of paradise on it and I'll read you a story
from that book you're always after. And now, are you still glad
to be leaving me?

JANE. Not at all Bessie. Indeed just now I am rather sad.

BESSIE. 'Just now' and 'rather'. How coolly she says it. I dare
say if I were to ask you for a kiss you'd say you'd rather not.

JANE. Bend your head down.

BESSIE *bends her head and* JANE *kisses her awkwardly then turns away embarrassed.* BESSIE *kisses* JANE *warmly on the cheek.* BESSIE *takes* JANE's *school apron and bonnet from her basket and dresses her.*

JANE (*excited*). At school I shall learn to draw and write stories and speak in foreign languages. I shall work hard and be helpful and friendly and never . . .

We hear the sound of BERTHA *whining, her face pushed into the crack in the door.* JANE *and* BESSIE *hug. The scene is broken by the sound of a bell.*

Scene 3

Lowood School. Assembly. JANE *stands on a high stool.*

BROCKLEHURST. I place her thus so that everyone may see her and recognise her. You observe she possesses the ordinary form of childhood. No one would think that the evil one has already found a servant and agent in her yet such is the case. This girl is not a true member of the flock. You must shun her example. Avoid her company. Teachers, you must keep your eyes on her movements and weigh well her words, for in these words is her illness. (*Sees a girl in the audience.*) This girl is a liar. What is that girl with curled hair? Curled red hair. Stand up. Turn around. Why has she or any other curled hair? I have again and again said that hair must be arranged modestly, plainly . . .

TEACHER. Her hair curls naturally, sir.

BROCKLEHURST. Naturally! We are here to mortify in these girls the lusts of the flesh. To teach them to clothe themselves with shamefacedness and sobriety. That girl's hair. It must be cut off entirely. I will send a barber tomorrow.

A bell rings.

(*Looking at* JANE.) Let her stand half an hour longer.

The children disperse. JANE *stands frozen. As soon as she is alone she slumps and dissolves into tears. A moment later she sees through the mists the figure of* HELEN BURNS. *She is wearing the untidy badge and holding out a cup of water.* JANE *takes it and drinks.* HELEN *sets down a bucket of water and scours the floor.*

JANE. Why are you kind to a girl whom everyone believes to be a liar?

HELEN. Everyone? There are only eighty people who have heard you called so. The world contains hundreds of millions.

JANE. But what have I to do with millions? The eighty I know despise me.

HELEN. They pity you more like.

JANE. How can they pity me after what he . . .

HELEN. Mr Brocklehurst is not a God.

JANE. But he told them . . .

HELEN. Sssh.

JANE. He told them I . . .

HELEN. If all the world believed you wicked while your own conscience approved you, you would not be without friends.

BROCKLEHURST *enters.* HELEN *stands.*

BROCKLEHURST. Helen Burns. You will scrub the kitchen yard and wear the disobedience badge for the rest of the week. And you shall stay as you are an hour longer.

HELEN *curtsies.* BROCKLEHURST *leaves.* HELEN *continues to scrub the floor.*

Scene 4

JANE. You were right to say that Mr Brocklehurst is not a God. He is a tyrant.

HELEN. He does as he thinks best.

JANE. Do you not resent him and wish him ill for making you wear the disobedience badge and scrub the kitchen yard in the freezing . . .

HELEN. He is right. I am disobedient.

JANE. He is cruel and harsh. He should be punished, not you.

HELEN. He dislikes my faults.

JANE. But if good people are always obedient then wicked people will have it all their own way.

HELEN. Vengeance cannot heal injury.

JANE. Yes it can. When we are struck at unfairly we should strike back. Very hard.

HELEN. Would you not be happier if you tried to forget his severity?

JANE. Forget? How can I? He has . . .

HELEN. Life is too short to be spent nursing anger and counting up wrongs.

JANE. He has made all but you despise me and I cannot bear to be alone and hated. To gain affection I would willingly have the bone of my arm broken . . . or stand behind a kicking horse and let its hoof dash against my chest . . .

HELEN. Sssh, Jane. You think too much of the love of human beings.

JANE. But who else will . . .

HELEN. You are not alone nor ever will be. There is an invisible world, a kingdom of spirits, they watch over us, they are here to guide us. They see our torture and recognise our innocence. Why then be distressed when life is short and death certain entrance to happiness?

JANE looks around as if expecting to see a spirit. She falls to her knees and begins to pray fiercely. She says the Lord's Prayer as if her life depends on it.

Scene 5

It is evening some weeks later. A TEACHER *enters.* JANE *continues to pray.*

TEACHER. Jane Eyre, why are you still at prayer? Did you not hear the evening bell?

JANE. I'm sorry sir. I forgot the time.

TEACHER. Go quietly. Take off your shoes.

JANE. Sir, why was Helen not in class today?

TEACHER. She is unwell.

JANE. What makes her ill?

TEACHER. She has tuberculosis.

JANE. And Sarah? And Anne?

TEACHER. They are sick too.

JANE. Will they get better?

TEACHER. Maybe. If we pray for them. There will be no lessons for the rest of the week. You will spend your time at study and at prayer. The sickroom is out of bounds.

Scene 6

Several weeks later. It is late at night. JANE *stands in the entrance to the sickroom. There are rows of* GIRLS *lying beneath sheets.* HELEN BURNS *is amongst them. She senses* JANE.

HELEN. Jane? Is that you?

JANE. They said I might not come but I wanted to see you.

She goes to HELEN .

HELEN. Sssh. (*She takes* JANE's *hand*). You have come to wish me goodbye.

JANE. Are you going somewhere? Are you going home?

HELEN. Yes. To my last home. My long home.

JANE. No. No, Helen.

HELEN. Yes. I am sure of it.

JANE. But only last week you took a walk in the garden and . . .

HELEN (*coughs a while*). I am very happy Jane. When I am dead you must not grieve.

JANE. Where are you going to Helen? Can you see? Do you know?

HELEN. I am going to God.

JANE. You are sure then there is such a place as Heaven? That our souls will go there when we die and I shall see you again?

HELEN (*she coughs and lies back into* JANE's *arms*). How comfortable I am. I feel as if I could sleep, but don't leave me. I like to have you near me.

JANE. No one will take me away.

They lie together. JANE prays. The Lord's Prayer. They sleep. The GIRLS are entwined in each other's arms. The TEACHER enters. He sees that HELEN is dead. He closes her eyes. He lifts the sheet and covers her head. He continues the Lord's Prayer, lifting JANE in her sleep. JANE is carried away still half dreaming. She opens her eyes as she is taken from the room. Her arms reach out towards HELEN and she cries out. HELEN BURNS stands very slowly and walks towards a blinding light.

Scene 7

Seven years later. JANE is dressed in a full length grey frock. She is now a teacher at Lowood. Two GIRLS sit on a bench. The sheets that were used to create the beds in the sickroom are now being embroidered. It is a sewing class. JANE paces back and forth as she speaks.

JANE. The herringbone stitch is a decorative stitch used in the embroidery of handkerchiefs, linens and bonnets. The thread is brought forward from behind and fed back at a diagonal.

Suddenly she stops and speaks her thoughts. The GIRLS continue to sew.

JANE. Oh, how I long to see beyond that dreary hill. How I wish I could see into the busy world I have read about. Towns. Cities full of life and activity. Oh Lord, I know I should be contented. I am fed and clothed and have means to live. But is there not more to life?

She addresses the class, continuing to pace.

Using the thumb and forefinger, pull the thread tight enough to secure it but not so tight as to make a hole.

She stops and speaks her thoughts.

Of the whole wide world I know nothing but his tiny corner. Nothing but this endless round of dreary tasks, each day the same as the day before. Oh, Lord, forgive me, but I must know more.

The GIRLS disappear. JANE writes a letter and seals it, hugging it to herself.

Scene 8

The sound of horses' hooves and carriage wheels. It is one month later. JANE's luggage is being passed down from a carriage and carried away by a servant. She has arrived at Thornfield where MRS FAIRFAX, the housekeeper, awaits.

MRS FAIRFAX. Your hands are half numb from the cold. Come inside. I am so glad you are here. All winter we have seen no one but the butcher and the postman and then a month ago Adele arrived. She is Mr Rochester's ward. Her mother died, bless her, and so he has left her with me who cannot speak a word of her language, poor child. She must talk to herself in the mirror for company.

They enter the house met by ADELE who runs into the room breathless. She is a ten-year-old with ringlets and perfect deportment. She looks like a doll.

Come and speak to the lady who is to teach you and make you understand me.

ADELE. C'est la gouvernante!

JANE. Bonjour.

ADELE shakes her hand and curtsies.

ADELE. Vous parlez Français?

JANE. Oui.

ADELE. C'est magnifique.

She kisses JANE and then pirouettes across the floor.

Est-ce que vous aimez danser?

MRS FAIRFAX. Now, now. Be still. Miss Eyre is tired from her journey.

ADELE. Cela vous plait, mon bracelet? Il est joli, n'est-ce pas?

MRS FAIRFAX. Can you understand her when she runs on so fast?

JANE. I was taught by a French lady.

MRS FAIRFAX. Tell her it is time for bed.

JANE. Il faut aller vous coucher, maintenant. On se voit demain.

ADELE *curtsies like an actress at the end of a play and runs away calling.*

ADELE. A demain.

JANE. Mr Rochester is away?

MRS FAIRFAX. His visits to England are rare and always unexpected. He never stays for long. A week.

Maybe two.

A servant descends the staircase.

Here is Grace Poole. She will show you to your room.

JANE *and* GRACE *look at one another without exchanging a greeting.* GRACE *picks up* JANE'*s suitcase and leads her away.*

Scene 9

A month later. The school room. JANE *and* ADELE *are embroidering samplers.* ADELE *is restless and petulant. After a few moments she throws her sampler down.*

ADELE. Ah, c'est difficile.

JANE (*picking up sampler*). You have pulled it too tight. Look, you've nearly made a hole.

ADELE. C'est compliqué.

JANE. In English Adele. We speak English in class.

ADELE. I don't like to work today.

She gets up and jetés across the floor.

JANE. Unpick the stitches and start again.

ADELE. Regardez-moi!

She spins on tiptoe.

JANE. Adele.

ADELE. Look at me!

She spins again.

JANE. You may go. Lessons will continue this afternoon. Tell Cook I'm not hungry.

ADELE leaves. JANE picks up ADELE's sampler and tries to unpick the stitches. She pulls impatiently at the tangled thread making it worse. We hear BERTHA kicking against the floor in a distant room. It is the sound of a caged animal. This restlessness registers in JANE's body making it hard to stay still. She tries to use the embroidery to control her agitation but it increases as if some force were coming through her. Finally she throws the sampler down and gets up.

JANE. Oh Lord forgive me. I know that women are supposed to be calm. I know that women should be satisfied with tranquility but it is not so. Women feel just as men feel. They suffer from stagnation. They must not confine themselves to making puddings and knitting stockings and playing the piano. They must exercise their powers. They must have action, and they will make it if they cannot find it.

The kicking feet grow louder and louder and take on the rhythm of a galloping horse. We hear the sound of hooves on a rocky road magnified in the imagination. We see behind her ROCHESTER on a horse, galloping towards us through the mist. His dog, PILOT runs ahead. Suddenly the horse rears up slipping on the ice. ROCHESTER falls in front of JANE. The dog PILOT snarls violently at JANE.

JANE. Are you injured sir?

ROCHESTER. What the deuce . . .

JANE. Can I do anything?

ROCHESTER (*to* PILOT). Shut up! (*To* JANE.) You can get out of my way.

He tries to struggle to his feet.

JANE. If you are hurt and want help I can fetch someone from Thornfield.

ROCHESTER. Stand aside. I've no broken bones, only a sprain. Here boy.

He calls to the horse who is frisky and wary. The dog barks.

Thornfield you say?

JANE. That is where I live. Just below. I was going to post a letter but I can . . .

ROCHESTER. Whose house is it?

JANE. Mr Rochester's.

ROCHESTER. Indeed.

JANE. Do you know Mr Rochester?

ROCHESTER. Very well. You are not a servant at the hall. You are
. . . (*Realising.*) Of course, you are . . .

JANE. I am the governess.

ROCHESTER. I had forgotten. The governess. In that case you
may help me a little yourself if you would. Get hold of my
horse's bridle and lead him to me.

*JANE walks towards the horse slowly. She is afraid but
determined. She tries to catch the bridle but the horse rears up
and backs away. She is afraid of the horse's feet.*

ROCHESTER (*laughing*). I see. Then I must beg you to come
here.

She goes to him.

Necessity compels me to make you useful.

*He lays his hand on her shoulder and she helps him hobble
towards the horse. He mounts with difficulty.*

Tell your Mr Rochester that young ladies ought not to be
wandering abroad on such a night.

JANE. I was not wandering sir. I was, as I said, going to post a
letter

ROCHESTER. Then make haste and return as fast as you can.

He is gone.

Scene 10

*Half an hour later. JANE is met by MRS FAIRFAX at the door.
MRS FAIRFAX is carrying ROCHESTER's coat.*

MRS FAIRFAX. You are back, thank goodness! Did you ever see
snow fall so fast?

JANE. Whose is that coat?

MRS FAIRFAX. The master's. He's just now arrived.

JANE. The master?

MRS FAIRFAX. Mr Rochester. He's had a fall on the ice and sprained his ankle.

PILOT, ROCHESTER's dog, comes bounding down the hallway. He recognises JANE and goes to lick her fingers as MRS FAIRFAX hurries away. JANE crouches beside him and strokes his head.

She looks up to see GRACE POOLE coming towards her. She is carrying a tray laid out for a meal with a lighted candle. JANE stands.

JANE. Good evening.

GRACE nods her head and continues on up the stairs.

Scene 11

The schoolroom, the following day. JANE is teaching ADELE to read the Lord's Prayer. ADELE is excited by MR ROCHESTER's recent arrival. JANE too is full of curiosity but tries to concentrate on the lesson.

ADELE. 'Our Father . . . Who art in . . . ' Je connais pas ce mot-là.

JANE. In English Adele.

ADELE. I forget.

JANE. 'Heaven'.

ADELE. Qu'est-ce que vous pensez que Monsieur Rochester m'a acheté?

JANE (*pointing at the words*). 'Our Father, Who art in Heaven . . . ' Repeat.

ADELE. 'Our Father, Who are in Heaven . . . ' I asked for a dress. Like the swan in Swan Lake. With . . . Ah . . . qu'est-ce que c'est, le mot en anglais: Les ailes.

JANE. Wings.

ADELE. Wings.

She gets up and 'flies', using her arms for wings in imitation of the ballet which she has seen and remembered. JANE closes the book giving in to her curiosity.

JANE. Where has Mr Rochester come from?

ADELE. From Paris and Rome and before that, another place.
Perhaps he brings you also a cadeau. He asked me the name of
my gouvernante and if you are small and pale and thin and I
said yes.

JANE (*opening her book swiftly*). 'Our Father, Who art in
Heaven . . . '

ADELE. 'Our Father, Who art in Heaven . . . '

JANE. Continue.

MRS FAIRFAX *enters.*

MRS FAIRFAX. Mr Rochester requests you and your pupil to
come to the drawing room.

Scene 12

The drawing room. ROCHESTER *sits in an armchair with* PILOT
at his side, his foot in a bandage. ADELE, MRS FAIRFAX *and*
JANE *enter.* ADELE *looks for the box of presents.*

ROCHESTER. I see Adele is disappointed. She had expected to
see a pile of presents and finds only myself and Pilot. A poor
substitute.

ADELE. Good evening.

She curtsies.

ROCHESTER. They will be delivered next week.

ADELE. How is your ankle?

ROCHESTER. You have done well Miss Eyre. Your pupil is
neither bright nor disciplined and yet she has made progress.

JANE. Thank you.

ROCHESTER. Come out of the shadows. I cannot see you.

JANE *reluctantly moves a little forward into the light but does
not look at* ROCHESTER. ADELE *takes* PILOT *into a corner.*

Where did you come from?

JANE. Lowood School.

ROCHESTER. You were a pupil?

JANE. And then a teacher. For two years.

ROCHESTER. Your parents?

JANE. Dead sir.

ROCHESTER. Brothers and sisters?

JANE. I have none.

ROCHESTER. I thought not.

Pause.

When you came upon me last night I thought of sprites in fairy tales. I had half a mind you had bewitched my horse.

MRS FAIRFAX *passes him a glass of brandy.*

Who recommended you to come here?

JANE. I advertised . . . and Mrs Fairfax answered. It was the only reply.

MRS FAIRFAX. Miss Eyre has been a valuable companion to me and an excellent teacher to Adele.

ROCHESTER. Don't trouble yourself to give her a good reference. I shall judge for myself. She began by felling my horse.

MRS FAIRFAX (*confused*). Sir?

ROCHESTER. Adele has shown me some of your drawings. I was intrigued. I take it they are borne of the imagination. You have not yourself travelled the world?

We become aware of BERTHA *stretching.*

JANE. No, sir.

ROCHESTER. You have been tutored though I see.

JANE. No, sir.

ROCHESTER. Then you have some natural talent.

JANE. I . . . cannot say.

ROCHESTER. And whyever not?

JANE. I have no means by which to judge.

ROCHESTER. You mean you have nothing to compare it with.
    You have seen little of society and less of culture. Am I right?

JANE. Yes, sir.

ROCHESTER. I see you are fascinated by the pattern in my carpet. My questions are a trial to you. You may leave, and take Adele with you. Next time you will not escape so easily. Goodnight.

Minutes later in the hallway. ADELE *has gone to bed.* MRS FAIRFAX *undoes her apron.*

JANE. You said that Mr Rochester was gentlemanly and kind.

MRS FAIRFAX. And so he is.

JANE. He is abrupt . . . and changeful.

MRS FAIRFAX. I am so accustomed to his manner I never think of it.

JANE. He blows hot and then cold in the space of a moment.

MRS FAIRFAX. If he is sometimes ill-tempered allowances should be made.

JANE. Why?

MRS FAIRFAX (*hesitates*). He has painful thoughts.

JANE. What about?

MRS FAIRFAX. Family troubles I believe.

JANE. What kind . . .

MRS FAIRFAX. Don't ask me for details, I know none. He has never spoken of it . . .

We hear a stifled laugh. It is BERTHA.

JANE. Who is that?

MRS FAIRFAX. Grace Poole. She sleeps in the attic. I shall tell her to be quiet. She has forgotten the master is at home.

JANE. Grace Poole!

MRS FAIRFAX. She has had something to drink. It is a weakness of hers.

MRS FAIRFAX *leaves. The laugh is heard once more.* JANE *listens.*

Scene 13

The drawing room, the following evening. MR ROCHESTER *is seated as before.* JANE *and* ADELE *enter.* ADELE *immediately sees a large box of presents which she runs to.*

ADELE. Mes boîtes! Mes boîtes!

ROCHESTER. Drag them into a corner and amuse yourself disembowelling them. Mind you don't bother me with its entrails.

> ADELE *runs to him kissing him and then takes the box to a corner as bid.*

Miss Eyre. Is she there?

JANE. I am sir.

ROCHESTER. Be seated.

> *He indicates a chair opposite his. She sits, pulling the chair backwards out of the light.*

Don't draw the chair away Miss Eyre. Sit down where I place it.

> MRS FAIRFAX *enters.*

Mrs Fairfax, I sent to you for a charitable purpose. I have forbidden Adele to talk to me about her presents. Have the goodness to serve as her audience.

> *Pause.*

I am disposed to be gregarious tonight Miss Eyre. Talk to me.

> *Pause.*

JANE. What about sir?

ROCHESTER. Whatever you like. I leave the choice of subject entirely to yourself.

> *Silence.*

You are silent. You think me insolent. You think I have no right to command you in such a way. I read as much in your eye. Beware what you express with that organ Miss Eyre. I am an expert at reading its language.

> JANE *looks away. He studies her.*

I am old enough to be your father. I have roamed half the globe and seen much of life. Does that not allow me to be a little commanding, a little masterful once in a while?

JANE (*shyly*). You may do as you please.

ROCHESTER. That is no answer.

JANE. I don't think, sir, you have the right to command me merely because you are older than I or because you have seen more of the world. Your claim to superiority depends on the use you have made of your experience. I am, however, paid to receive your orders.

ROCHESTER. Paid! Paid! I had forgotten the salary. Well, on that mercenary ground do you agree to let me hector you a little?

JANE (*softening*). No, sir. Not on that ground . . . but on the ground that you did forget the salary.

She looks him in the eye.

ROCHESTER. I may dispense with conventionalities then. You will not think me insolent?

JANE. I shall never mistake informality for insolence. One I rather like. The other nothing free born would submit to.

ADELE *has opened the parcel containing her dress.*

ADELE. Oh regardez! C'est belle. C'est magnifique.

MRS FAIRFAX. Ssssh.

ADELE. Il faut que je l'essaie. Attendez. Je reviens. Come with me.

She takes MRS FAIRFAX's *hand and leads her out of the room.*

JANE *and* ROCHESTER *are alone.*

ROCHESTER. You examine me Miss Eyre. Do you think me handsome?

JANE. No. (*She looks away.*)

ROCHESTER. You say little but when you do it is to the point.

JANE. Sir I was too plain. I ought to have replied that beauty is of little consequence.

ROCHESTER. You ought to have replied no such thing. Beauty of no consequence indeed. Under the pretence of softening the previous outrage you stick the knife in further.

JANE. It is late. I see I have outstayed my welcome.

She stands.

ROCHESTER. Wait. In a moment Adele will return in her costume. She will be a miniature of her mother. My tenderest feelings are about to receive a shock.

Pause.

Have you ever loved, Miss Eyre?

He looks at her.

I think not. Your eye is still clear. Your brow smooth.

Pause.

You may find it hard to believe but I was once like you. My memory unpolluted. My conscience clean. A memory unsoiled is an exquisite treasure. A source of pure refreshment.

ADELE *runs in dressed in her swan tutu complete with tiny wings.*

ADELE. Monsieur, I thank you a thousand times for your kindness.

She does a few steps of a dance she learned from her maman. Her movements are beguiling and flirtatious. She showers ROCHESTER *with kisses and then drops to her knee at his feet, pleased with herself.*

I do exactly like Maman n'est-ce pas?

ROCHESTER. Precisely.

He is momentarily transfixed and then shakes himself as if from a daydream.

(*Furious.*) It is nine o'clock. What are you about Miss Eyre to let Adele stay up so late. Take her to bed.

ADELE *goes to kiss him goodnight and then runs away in tears.* JANE *curtsies and is about to leave when* ROCHESTER *stops her. During the following speech we hear snatches of* BERTHA*'s West Indian rain song far away and see* BERTHA *lying on the attic floor. She rolls over and stretches like a cat in the sunshine. She strokes her face and arms.*

ROCHESTER. Do you never laugh Miss Eyre? Don't trouble to answer. I see you laugh rarely. The Lowood constraint still clings to you, muffles your voice, controls your features and limbs. You fear to speak too freely or move too quickly, but in time you will be natural with me. I find it impossible to be conventional with you.

Pause.

You are still bent on going?

JANE. You ordered me to do so sir.

ROCHESTER. So I did. I had forgotten. Goodnight.

She walks quickly away. As soon as she is alone she touches her face. She feels her features with her fingers. A smile steals across her face. She turns slowly, listening to BERTHA's song. We see BERTHA above, arms outstretched and head thrown back. She too turns slowly. It recalls the rain dance of the first scene but less abandoned. Like a memory of a dance she once knew. It is the moment when the rain comes and she drinks. BERTHA begins to laugh. The sound startles JANE, awakening her from her reverie. She kneels to say her prayers: the 'Our Father'. She uses the prayer to suppress her feelings of excitement.

Scene 14

Several weeks later. It is a warm spring evening. ADELE and JANE are playing ball. JANE looks happier, more relaxed. Her clothes are loosened for out of doors. ADELE is less doll-like, running like a child and forgetting her appearance. PILOT appears with his master. The ball is dropped and he retrieves it, returning it to ROCHESTER.

ROCHESTER. Adele. You must allow me to steal your playmate on the grounds that I give you mine. Go boy.

He throws the ball for PILOT to fetch.

JANE. What a beautiful evening. It's like Summer already.

ROCHESTER. She is quite transformed by your efforts.

JANE. She has begun to be interested in her lessons. I caught her reading a book of her own accord yesterday.

They watch her a while.

ROCHESTER. Do you see any likeness in her to me?

JANE. No. Why, should I?

ROCHESTER. Her mother insisted she was my daughter. I cannot see it for myself . . .

Pause.

You are shocked?

JANE. I understood she was no relation.

ROCHESTER. You may well be right. Her mother was a French dancer. I was, I believed, deeply in love. I lavished her with gifts. Set her up in her own apartment. Then, one night I decided to surprise her with a visit. I waited on her balcony. She returned from the theatre with another man. I was forced to listen to their whisperings and lovemaking.

Pause.

You never felt jealousy, did you, Miss Eyre. Of course not. You have never felt love. Your soul sleeps. You float on downstream with closed eyes and muffled ears. But I tell you, one day it will happen. You will be dragged helpless into the rapids. You will be tossed and crushed and flung. Either you will be dashed to pieces or lifted up and borne by some great wave into a calmer current, as I am now.

Pause.

On a day like today I might almost believe myself happy.

JANE. You find Thornfield tranquil. It pleases you to be here?

ROCHESTER. *Now* it does. In the past I abhorred the very thought of it.

PILOT *brings* ROCHESTER *the ball. He hides it behind his back and then throws it to* ADELE. *She runs off with* PILOT *following her, barking wildly.*

You will perhaps think differently now of your protégé. You will be coming to me soon with notice that you've found a new situation and wish to be replaced.

JANE. No. Adele is not answerable for her mother's faults or yours. Now that I know she is an orphan I shall cling to her closer than before.

ROCHESTER. And what of me?

JANE. Sir?

ROCHESTER. Do you regard me as irredeemable now you know something of my past.

JANE. No, sir, (*Tentatively.*) because you are living now I think by better rules.

ROCHESTER. But how can I clear the dark pool of memory. Can I live again without remorse and guilt?

JANE. Repentance, sir, is the cure they say.

ROCHESTER (*laughs mockingly*). Of course.

JANE. If from this day forward you decide to correct your thoughts and actions you will soon have a new store of recollections. One to which you might revert with pleasure.

ROCHESTER (*with intensity*). Yes. Indeed.

Pause.

I believe it to be so. It must be so.

He looks at JANE *long and hard. She cannot fathom his thoughts but feels the intensity and cannot speak. The sky darkens.*

She breaks from him suddenly. She becomes very formal.

JANE. I must go sir.

ROCHESTER. Of course.

JANE. Mrs Fairfax will be waiting.

ROCHESTER. Indeed.

JANE. And Adele.

ROCHESTER. Yes.

JANE. Good evening.

ROCHESTER. Good evening.

JANE hurries away. As soon as she is alone she falls to her knees and speaks to God. During this sequence BERTHA *is playing with the flame of a candle, lighting paper and watching it burn.* GRACE *is with her, sleeping in her chair.*

JANE. Forgive me Lord. Teach me to be calm. To want nothing. Desire nothing for myself.

Scene 15

JANE *lies down to sleep but begins to heave and murmur. She is having a sexual dream.* BERTHA *steals across the attic carrying the candle. The keys to the door are in* GRACE's *pocket. She must steal them without waking her. Every time* JANE *cries out it sends a spasm through* BERTHA.

JANE. I want . . . I want to . . . Let me . . .

> *These words are scarcely audible but suggest a conflict happening in the dream.* BERTHA, *after several attempts finally teases the keys from* GRACE's *pocket. She runs to the door. We hear the sound of the locks opening. It is as if* JANE *is released. She murmurs with pleasure.* GRACE *is woken by the noise. As* BERTHA *disappears through the door she starts after her.* BERTHA *carries the flame aloft. She enters* ROCHESTER's *chamber. She straddles his sleeping body, bearing down on him in an expression of lust and rage.* JANE's *movements echo* BERTHA's. GRACE *finally catches up with* BERTHA *and lays hold of her. She wrestles her backwards and drops the candle.* JANE *awakes with a start.* BERTHA *is forced back up the stairs.* JANE *comes out into the passageway. She sees the dropped candle and then smells fire. She runs to* ROCHESTER's *room beating back the smoke and covering her mouth. She grabs a pitcher of water and throws it over* ROCHESTER *drenching him. He wakes confused.*

ROCHESTER. Is there a flood?

JANE. No, sir. There has been a fire.

ROCHESTER. Is that Jane Eyre? Have you plotted to drown me?

JANE. No, sir. But someone has tried to burn you alive. Your sheets were on fire. A minute later you would have . . .

ROCHESTER. Wait here. (*He hurries up to the attic and centres with* GRACE *who is locking the door. He returns to* JANE.) What did you see on quitting your chamber?

JANE. A candle, dropped on the floor. And I heard footsteps on the stairs leading to the attic. There is a woman who sews here. Grace Poole. She sleeps in the attic does she not?

ROCHESTER. Yes yes, indeed, you have guessed it. I have my own reasons for keeping her here. You are no talking fool Jane.

Say nothing about tonight's incident. I will account for it in the morning. Now, return to your room.

JANE. But Grace Poole is still . . .

ROCHESTER. Have no fear. I can take care of myself.

Pause.

JANE. Goodnight then sir.

ROCHESTER. What, are you quitting me already?

JANE. You said I might go.

ROCHESTER. But not without taking leave. You have saved my life, snatched me from a horrible death and you walk past me as if we were strangers. At least shake hands.

She does so. He takes her hand in both of his.

Nothing else that has being would have been tolerable to me as a creditor. But you, I knew you would come good in some way. I saw it in your eyes when I first beheld you. Their expression did not . . . did not strike delight to my very inmost heart for nothing.

JANE (*removing her hand*). I am glad I happened to be awake.

She goes to leave.

ROCHESTER. What? Will you go?

JANE. I am cold sir.

He takes his coat and wraps it around her shoulders. He lingers a moment and then snatches his hands away.

ROCHESTER. Cold, yes. And standing in a puddle. Go then Jane. Go.

She goes to her room. She is suddenly aware of the sensation of his coat around her. She smells it. It smells of him. She wraps it around herself and then takes it in her arms nestling into its soft folds as if it were alive. BERTHA, now restored to her room, caresses the door with a deep sense of longing.

Scene 16

The next day. ADELE, MRS FAIRFAX *and* JANE *are eating lunch.* JANE *has barely eaten.*

MRS FAIRFAX. Now Miss Eyre, eat up. You ate so little at breakfast I am afraid you are not well today.

ADELE (*frightened*). The curtains are burned to ashes. The walls and windows are black with smoke. Imagine if Mr Rochester did not awake.

MRS FAIRFAX. I do hope in future you will pay attention, Jane. I know that you too are fond of reading in bed with a candle.

ADELE. The sheets were burned black at the edges. A minute longer and he would have been . . .

MRS FAIRFAX (*changing the subject*). Thank goodness the sun shone today and he has had good weather for his journey.

JANE. Journey?

MRS FAIRFAX. He is gone to South Leas. I believe there is quite a party there.

JANE. Do you expect him back tonight?

MRS FAIRFAX. No. Not for two weeks or more.

MRS FAIRFAX *smiles to herself.*

And there is a certain young lady he will no doubt be pleased to see.

JANE. Who is that?

MRS FAIRFAX. You have heard perhaps of Blanche Ingram. She is known hereabouts as something of a beauty and indeed lives up to her reputation.

JANE. You have seen her. What is she like?

As BLANCHE *is described she appears, running into the middle of the 'table' space, laughing and fanning herself.* MR ROCHESTER *follows.*

MRS FAIRFAX. Elegant with a fine figure and beautiful dark eyes. Altogether a pleasure to look upon. Talented too. She plays the piano and sings. She and Mr Rochester sang a duet together.

JANE. Mr Rochester! I was not aware he could sing.

MRS FAIRFAX. Oh yes. He has a fine bass voice.

BLANCHE *begins to sing and is joined by* MR ROCHESTER. *They look into each others' eyes.*

JANE (*suddenly getting up*). Excuse me. I'm afraid you were right Mrs Fairfax. I am feeling unwell.

She pushes ROCHESTER *and* BLANCHE *aside. The image disappears. She runs into her bedroom.*

BERTHA *is seen still caressing the locked door and murmuring. During the following speech her movements become gradually more violent and contorted, expressing a sense of sexual guilt and self hatred.*

JANE. A greater fool than Jane Eyre never breathed the breath of life. *You*, a favourite with Mr Rochester? *You*, gifted with the power of pleasing him. *You*, of importance to him in any way?

She picks up the mirror.

He said something in praise of your eyes did he? Well, look at those eyes.

She forces herself to look at her reflection.

Look at that tired, uneven, charmless face and draw it with chalk onto a piece of paper. Write under it 'Portrait of a governess. Disconnected, poor and plain'. Afterwards, mix your finest tints and paint the loveliest face you can imagine according to Mrs Fairfax's description. Whenever in future you should fancy Mr Rochester thinks well of you, take out those two pictures and compare them.

Pause.

I will do it.

Scene 17

The image as before of MR ROCHESTER *and* BLANCHE *singing together floats through the sea of activity. Everything arrives in its place just as it is wanted so that the party arrives in a semi circle around* ROCHESTER *and* BLANCHE *just as drinks and delicacies are being served.* ADELE *is amongst the guests. When the song finishes the audience clap.* MRS FAIRFAX *leaves the party and goes to* JANE *who sits in her room reading her Bible.*

MRS FAIRFAX (*pleased for* JANE). Mr Rochester has requested your company in the drawing room.

JANE. He does so out of politeness. I need not go I'm sure.

MRS FAIRFAX. I told him I thought you would decline and he told me to tell you it was his particular wish and if you resist further to say he will come and fetch you.

JANE (*closing the Bible*). I will not give him that trouble.

ADELE *has taken the floor and finishes a song learnt from her mama.* JANE *slips in and sits a distance away from the company in the forestage sewing her sampler.* ADELE *bows and receives much applause and petting. The actors should play these scenes as if surrounded by invisible guests to create the illusion of a party.*

LORD INGRAM. What a poppet. Beautifully sung.

BLANCHE. Mr Rochester I thought you were not fond of children.

ROCHESTER. Nor am I.

BLANCHE. You should send her to school.

ROCHESTER. She has a governess.

BLANCHE. Oh yes. I think I saw such a person just now. Very miserable she looked.

LORD INGRAM. My dearest do not mention governesses. The very word makes me nervous. Thank heavens I have done with them. (*Drops his voice.*) I noticed yours just now and see in her all the faults of her class.

ROCHESTER (*aloud*). And what are they sir?

LORD INGRAM. I will tell you later.

ROCHESTER. But my curiosity will be past its appetite. It craves food now.

BLANCHE. I have just one word to say of the whole tribe. They are a nuisance. Not that we ever suffered much. (*Giggles.*)

LORD INGRAM. What tricks you used to play on ours!

BLANCHE. Miss Wilson was a poor sickly thing, not worth the trouble of provoking. Miss Gray was completely insensible, no blow ever took effect on her. But poor Madame Joubert! I remember her rages when we had driven her insane. Spilt our tea. Crumbled our cake and tossed our books up to the ceiling. Papa, do you remember those merry days?

LORD INGRAM. To crown it all she took the liberty of falling in love with the boys' mathematics tutor.

BLANCHE. Dear Papa, as soon as he got an inkling, he dismissed them both without payment.

LORD INGRAM. Certainly my own, and I was quite right. It is . . .

BLANCHE. Oh, Papa. Spare us the details, please. Let's change the subject.

LORD INGRAM. Quite right, my lily flower. Let us not waste our breath.

BLANCHE. Mr Rochester, another song. Mind you sing with spirit though.

ROCHESTER. You will forgive me if I cannot live up to the brilliance of my accomplice?

BLANCHE. Take care. If you don't please me I will shame you by showing you how things should be done.

ROCHESTER. What a promise! Now I shall endeavour to fail.

She sings. JANE *slips away seemingly unnoticed. She stops in the hallway to tie her shoelace. At this moment* ROCHESTER *enters into the song.* JANE *is transfixed by the beautiful sound of his voice. We become aware of* BERTHA *listening and drinking in the sound, her ear to the floorboards.*

The party vanishes and MR ROCHESTER *appears beside* JANE.

The music continues to play.

ROCHESTER. How do you do?

JANE (*startled*). I am very well sir.

ROCHESTER. Why did you not come and speak to me?

JANE. I . . . did not wish to disturb you. You seemed engaged sir.

ROCHESTER. What have you been doing during my absence?

JANE. Teaching Adele, as usual.

ROCHESTER. And getting a good deal paler as I saw at first sight. What is the matter?

JANE. Nothing at all sir.

ROCHESTER. Did you take any cold that night you half drowned me?

JANE. Not the least.

ROCHESTER. Return to the drawing room. You are deserting too early.

JANE. I am tired sir.

ROCHESTER. And depressed. What about? Tell me.

JANE. Nothing . . . Nothing sir. I am not depressed.

ROCHESTER. But you are. So much so that a few more words would bring tears to your eyes. Indeed they are there now.

JANE turns to hide her face.

Very well. Tonight you are excused but understand that so long as my visitors remain you will be expected to appear in the drawing room with Adele. Goodnight my . . .

He hesitates. BLANCHE enters. She is furious.

BLANCHE. Mr Rochester. We thought you must have been stricken with a fever. What other excuse could there be for abandoning a young lady in the middle of a . . .

ROCHESTER (*abruptly*). You must excuse me. I have to be up early. I am afraid tomorrow I must leave you. I have to make a trip on business which cannot be delayed.

He kisses BLANCHE's hand, bows and leaves. BLANCHE stares after him, perplexed.

Scene 18

The next day. BLANCHE flops in an armchair. She is listless and irritable. LORD INGRAM and ADELE are playing cards.

LORD INGRAM. Sweetheart, come and join us. We are short of a player.

BLANCHE. You know I cannot bear to play cards and never could.

LORD INGRAM. But we miss your company. You have hardly said a word all day. I do hope you aren't sickening for something.

Papa feels BLANCHE'*s forehead.* BLANCHE *pushes his hand away. At that moment the door bell rings.* ADELE *runs to the window.*

ADELE. C'est Monsieur Rochester déjà?

BLANCHE *also darts to the window. They peer out into the misty afternoon.*

BLANCHE (*furious*). It is a man. A stranger. How provoking. (*To* ADELE.) You tiresome monkey. (*To* JANE.) Should she not be sent to bed?

ADELE. It is only five o'clock in the afternoon.

BLANCHE. Five o'clock. Is that all?

MRS FAIRFAX *enters the room with a man of about forty-five. He has tanned skin and a trace of a foreign accent.*

MRS FAIRFAX. Allow me to introduce Mr Mason. A friend of Mr Rochester's from his time in . . .

MASON. Spanish Town, Jamaica. Forgive me, I come at an inopportune moment. I arrive from a very long journey. I must presume so far as to install myself here until Mr Rochester returns.

MRS FAIRFAX *takes his coat.*

GUESTS. Good evening.

LORD INGRAM. Perhaps Mr Mason will be our fourth player. We find ourselves short.

MASON. Forgive me if I decline. I must sit a while on top of the fire. I am half frozen.

MASON *takes a seat next to the fire, not far from* JANE. MRS FAIRFAX *enters and whispers something into* LORD INGRAM'*s ear.*

LORD INGRAM. Tell her she shall be put in the stocks if she does not take herself off.

BLANCHE. What is it?

LORD INGRAM. A tiresome old woman. A gypsy who is badgering to tell our fortunes.

ADELE. A gypsy.

BLANCHE. What is she like?

MRS FAIRFAX. A shockingly ugly creature Miss. And dirty as a crock.

BLANCHE. A real sorceress! What fun! Bring her in.

MRS FAIRFAX *exits.*

LORD INGRAM. My dear! Whatever are you thinking of? I cannot possibly . . .

BLANCHE. Indeed, Papa, but you can and you will. I wish to hear my fortune told.

ADELE. And me! And me!

LORD INGRAM. My best, my dearest! She may be a thief or a murderer.

ADELE *looks serious and sits back down.* MRS FAIRFAX *enters.*

MRS FAIRFAX. She refuses now to come in and insists on a room of her own. Those who wish to consult her must go to her one at a time.

LORD INGRAM. You see, my dear. She encroaches on our very being.

BLANCHE. Show her to the library. I shall go first.

BLANCHE *exits with* MRS FAIRFAX.

LORD INGRAM. Oh, my goodness. Mrs Fairfax, stand outside the door. If you hear so much as a squeak, call the servants.

He paces up and down. The rest of the party sit, a little nervous.

ADELE. Who shall go next? What shall I ask her? Do you think she can really see into the future?

MASON *warms his hands on the fire.*

JANE. You are warmer now I hope.

MASON. A little. I am not yet used to the climate. When I left the West Indies it was midsummer.

JANE. I knew Mr Rochester had travelled but I didn't know he had roamed so far.

MASON. Indeed. He lived some years in Jamaica and was quite settled there at one time.

BLANCHE *enters the room. Her face is pale and cool. She walks stiffly to her seat and picks up her book.*

ADELE. What happened?

LORD INGRAM. What did she say?

BLANCHE. Very little.

ADELE. Is she a real fortune teller?

LORD INGRAM. How do you feel?

BLANCHE (*haughtily*). You seem all of you to believe we have a genuine witch in the house. I have seen a gypsy vagabond. She told me just what such people usually tell. And now I think Papa will do well to put her in the stocks tomorrow morning as he threatened.

ADELE. Me next. Me next.

ADELE *runs from the room.*

LORD INGRAM. My darling. I told you not to go. It has made you unhappy. What did she say? Nasty old gypsy.

BLANCHE (*sharply*). She has not made me unhappy. She has not the power to make me unhappy. She is a charlatan and that is the end of it.

MRS FAIRFAX (*entering*). The gypsy requests that after the young lady she might see the governess. She seems to know your name and would insist upon it. I told her I would ask.

Scene 19

ADELE *exits from the library in fits of giggles.* JANE *enters and waits. We see an old* GYPSY WOMAN *hunched and swaddled in shawls, her face hidden from view.*

GYPSY. You want your fortune told?

JANE. I came out of curiosity. I have no faith.

GYPSY. It is like your impudence to say so. I heard it in your step as you crossed the hall.

JANE. You have a quick ear.

GYPSY. And eye. And brain.

JANE. You need them in your trade.

GYPSY. Especially with customers like you. Why don't you tremble?

JANE. I am not cold.

GYPSY. Why don't you turn pale?

JANE. I am not sick.

GYPSY. Why don't you ask for my art?

JANE. I am not silly.

GYPSY. You are cold, you are sick and you are silly.

JANE. Prove it.

GYPSY. You are cold because you are alone. No contact lights the fire that is within you. You are sick because the best of feelings, the highest and sweetest given to man is not known to you. You are silly because suffer as you may you will not reach towards the thing that you crave.

JANE. I don't understand enigmas. I never understood a riddle in my life.

GYPSY. Is there not one of the party here at Thornfield that you study? One whose movements you follow with curiosity?

JANE. I like to observe all the faces and all the figures.

BERTHA *is heard pacing her cell.*

GYPSY. You have no favourite?

JANE. It is as I say.

GYPSY. You must then be aware of the growing love between Mr Rochester and Blanche Ingram.

JANE. I have heard it said they intend to marry.

JANE *moves across the room picking up on* BERTHA*'s restlessness.*

GYPSY. But you yourself do not perceive it?

JANE (*snaps*). It is not my business.

GYPSY. You must agree that appearances would warrant that conclusion?

JANE. Perhaps.

GYPSY. You are doubtful. Well maybe you have reason. I told her just now that Rochester's fortune was not half what she believed it to be. She became wonderous grave and would hear no more.

JANE. But I did not come to hear Mr Rochester's fortune. I came to hear my own and you have told me nothing.

GYPSY. Kneel down and let me see your face.

JANE does so. The GYPSY *takes her face in her hands. During the next speech her voice becomes more and more clearly that of* MR ROCHESTER.

Meanwhile MASON *opens the attic door. He sees his sister for the first time in twelve years. The beautiful* YOUNG WOMAN *he once knew is haggard and filthy. She hides behind a chair, terrified and excited. He moves slowly towards her.*

Reason sits firm and holds the reigns. She will not let the feelings have sway. The passions may rage. Desire may imagine wonderful things but judgement shall have the last word in every argument. Strong wind, earthquake, shock and fire may pass by but she shall follow that small voice called reason.

JANE (*realising*). Mr Rochester!

JANE pulls herself away. At the same moment we hear a heart rending cry followed by a scuffle and the slamming of the attic door. MASON *staggers down the steps from the attic and falls to the ground dragging himself forward and clutching his arm. He has been bitten. The wound is in exactly the place that* BERTHA *bit* JOHN REED *in Scene 1.* ROCHESTER *springs to his feet and runs out into the hallway, his disguise falling to the floor.* JANE *follows.*

Scene 20

The landing.

MASON. She has done for me.

ROCHESTER. My God! What are you doing here?

MASON. I thought she had recognised me.

ROCHESTER. That's enough. You were a fool to go in there alone. Jane.

JANE. Yes, sir.

She runs to fetch a basin of water. He presses his handkerchief to the wound. It is soon soaked with blood.

Do you turn sick at the sight of blood?

JANE. I think not.

ROCHESTER. Then hold this fast to the wound.

She does so. She dips the bloody handkerchief into the water and wrings it out. She mops the man's face and then places the dressing back on the arm during the following.

I must leave you in this room with this gentleman for an hour . . . maybe two. You will not speak to him on any pretext, and Richard, it will be at the peril of your life if you speak to her. I shall go to get a surgeon. We shall have you away from here by dawn.

MASON. Let her be taken care of Rochester. She knew not what she did. Let her be treated as tenderly as may be.

ROCHESTER. I do my best. And have done so. And will always.

JANE. But sir. Will Grace Poole live here still?

ROCHESTER. It is not a circumstance I am able to alter.

JANE. It seems to me your life is hardly safe while she . . .

ROCHESTER. I must away . . . Hear me Mason. If you so much as open your lips I will not be answerable for the consequences.

ROCHESTER *goes to leave, but hesitates at the door.*

ROCHESTER. You will forgive Jane, my prank.

JANE. Sir?

ROCHESTER. The gypsy.

JANE. Not until I have thought through every word and I'm sure I made no blunder.

ROCHESTER. Oh no. You were very sensible. Very correct as always. It is more likely it is I who has made a blunder.

JANE. You sir?

ROCHESTER. I don't know. I cannot tell.

MASON *groans.*

LORD INGRAM. What's happening?

ADELE. Has there been an accident? What is it Monsieur?

ROCHESTER. A servant has had a nightmare. That is all. There is no need for alarm.

The crowd disperses and JANE is left alone with the moaning, bloody patient. Every time she places the dressing on the wound it fills with blood. She washes it and replaces it again. This sequence should have the quality of a nightmare, as if the blood were endless and can never be stopped. We can hear BERTHA snarling still, like a dog that has been trapped in a corner but will not lie low. Finally, darkness. The sound of AUNT REED calling distractedly for JANE as she is wheeled forward in a bath chair.

MRS REED. Jane . . . Jane Eyre . . . I want to . . . I want to . . . Jane.

Scene 21

Gateshead. BESSIE greets JANE. She takes her hands and looks into her face.

BESSIE. It is you, is it Miss Jane? (*They embrace.*)

JANE. How is she?

BESSIE. She has been asking for you endlessly. Thank goodness you are come.

MRS REED (*calls*). Jane Eyre!

BESSIE. Her son committed suicide. She's had some sort of attack.

MRS REED. I have had more trouble with that child than anyone would believe. I declare she talked to me once like something mad or a fiend.

JANE. Why, Mrs Reed, did you hate her so?

MRS REED. She attacked my dear John. Bit him on the shoulder and drew blood. Is he there?

BESSIE. No Mrs Reed. Nor can be.

JANE. I'm sorry.

MRS REED. Who is that?

JANE. It is I Aunt Reed.

MRS REED. Who calls me that? (*She peers at* JANE.) You are like . . . why you are like . . . Jane Eyre. It is a mistake. I wished to see Jane Eyre and fancy a likeness where none exists.

JANE. It is she, Aunt.

MRS REED (*realising it is indeed* JANE). Is there no-one in the room but you?

JANE. Bessie is here.

MRS REED. Send her away.

> BESSIE *goes.*

Look in my reticule. Open it and take out the letter you see.

> JANE *does so.*

Read the letter to me.

JANE. 'Madam. You will have the goodness to send me the address of my niece Jane Eyre. It is my intention to adopt her and have her live with me as my daughter thereby relieving you of her care. John Eyre.'

> JANE *takes in the news.*

Why did I never hear of this?

MRS REED. Because I disliked you too much. The fury you once turned on me.

JANE. Dear Mrs Reed, think no more of it. Forgive me for my passionate nature, I was but a child.

MRS REED. I wrote and told him you had died of the typhus fever. You may act now as you please. Write and contradict me. Expose my falsehood. You were born to torment me. My last hour is wracked by recollection of a deed which but for you I would never have been tempted to commit.

JANE. If you could think no more of it Aunt. If you could think of me with kindness and forgiveness.

MRS REED. You have a very bad disposition Jane Eyre and one to this day I will never understand.

> JANE *runs from the room.* BERTHA *pummels the door.*

Scene 22

JANE *runs in circles around the stage, clutching her suitcase to her chest. Finally, she stops, out of breath. She looks about her. She is on the road to Thornfield. She breathes deeply, sees the familiar countryside, it is a warm summer's evening. A little way ahead she sees* MR ROCHESTER *sitting sketching. He holds his pencil up to measure the perspective.* JANE *is startled and tries to tiptoe away unseen. Without looking at her he speaks.*

ROCHESTER. Up to your old tricks again, I see.

> JANE *freezes. Her heart races.*

> You would not send for a carriage and arrive like a common mortal but must steal upon us by twilight like a fairy. What the deuce have you done with yourself for thirty days?

JANE. I have been with my aunt sir, who was buried yesterday.

ROCHESTER. I see.

JANE. I came as soon as I was able. I wrote to Mrs Fairfax.

ROCHESTER. So I hear. Twice a week. On Mondays and Fridays. Adele too has had her weekly feast of a letter whilst I have not heard a single word.

JANE. You have been in London sir.

ROCHESTER. I suppose you found that out by second sight?

JANE. Mrs Fairfax told me in a letter.

ROCHESTER. Of course. In a letter. And did she tell you what I went to do?

JANE. She did.

ROCHESTER. You must see the carriage I bought Jane. Mrs Rochester will look magnificent on her wedding day. I wish I was a little better matched to complete the picture. Tell me now fairy as you are, can't you give me a charm and make me handsome?

JANE. It would be past the power of magic.

ROCHESTER (*stung*). I had forgotten your tendency to speak the truth.

JANE. I meant sir . . . (*Suddenly.*) A loving eye is all the charm
needed. To such you are handsome enough . . . or rather your
sternness has a power beyond beauty.

Silence.

ROCHESTER. You wish to pass. I am in your way. Forgive me.

*They look at one another a moment before she passes swiftly
and walks away. As soon as she is out of sight she begins to
run, finally flinging her suitcase onto the ground. She is
alarmed and excited.* BERTHA *spins in a circle like a child
making itself dizzy. She lets out a cry of excitement.*

JANE. Oh Lord. Why does my heart beat as if it would leap from
my breast? When first I saw him I trembled. I could not speak
nor move and walked towards him I know not how. It was as if
my limbs were not my own. As if something spoke for me, in
spite of me. What made me say such things? He is not a ghost
and yet every nerve I have is unstrung. Oh Lord, what does it
mean?

Scene 23

The garden. A beautiful summer's evening. JANE, ROCHESTER
and ADELE *play.* PILOT *bounds around them.* MRS FAIRFAX
*sits knitting on a bench. There is a sense of growing warmth and
intimacy between* JANE *and* ROCHESTER. JANE *goes to the
bench and sits down beside* MRS FAIRFAX, *breathless and flushed.*

JANE. Have you ever known such wonderful weather, day in day
out?

MRS FAIRFAX. Not that I can remember.

JANE (*basking*). This is how it must be to live in Italy or . . . I
wish it would go on forever. (*Checks herself.*) Is there any news
of the wedding?

MRS FAIRFAX. Not a word. This morning I decided to ask him
right out but he answered with a joke and queer smile. I cannot
make him out.

JANE. Perhaps even once he is married he might keep us together,
you, Adele and I, somewhere under his protection where we
might see him sometimes.

MRS FAIRFAX. Perhaps.

Scene 24

*Later. The garden at sunset. JANE is alone. She drinks in the
lovely evening. She hears ROCHESTER approach and tries to
leave quietly, unseen. She wafts the air gently about her head as
if an insect passed her by. The insect flies on and settles on
ROCHESTER's arm. He inspects it with pleasure.*

ROCHESTER (*without appearing to have seen her*). Jane. Come
and look at this fellow. I never saw the like before in England.

*JANE is shy of being alone with ROCHESTER in the semi-
darkness and continues her retreat.*

Turning back on so lovely a night? Surely no one can wish to
go to bed. Come and sit a while.

*She comes to him and sits beside him on the bench. BERTHA
has her back to the attic door. She leans back and breathes
deeply, as if inhaling some exquisite fragrance through the
crack.*

ROCHESTER. Thornfield is pleasant in Summer, is it not?

JANE. Yes, sir.

ROCHESTER. You must have become attached to the house . . .
and some of those within it.

JANE. Yes.

ROCHESTER. Pity.

Pause.

It is always the way in this life. No sooner have you settled
than a voice calls you to rise and move on.

JANE. Must I move on sir?

ROCHESTER. I believe you must.

BERTHA *becomes anxious.*

JANE. Then you are going to be married?

ROCHESTER. Exactly. Precisely. Adele will be sent away to
school.

JANE. Soon sir?

ROCHESTER. Very soon.

JANE. I will advertise immediately.

ROCHESTER. There is no need. I have found you a position.

JANE. Thank you sir. I am sorry to give . . .

ROCHESTER. It is to undertake the education of the five
daughters of Mrs O'Gall of Connaught, Ireland.

JANE. Is it a long, long way off?

ROCHESTER. A girl of your sense will not object to the journey.

JANE. Not the journey . . . but the distance. And the sea too is a
barrier.

ROCHESTER. From what Jane?

JANE. From England and from Thornfield and . . .

ROCHESTER. Well?

JANE. From you sir.

BERTHA *is trying to open the door.*

ROCHESTER. You know Jane. Sometimes I have a queer feeling,
especially when you are near me such as now. It is as if I had a
string somewhere under my rib and every time you move or
speak I feel a tug. I am afraid that if you went to Connaught
that string would snap and I would bleed inwardly.

Pause.

As for you. You would forget me I suppose.

JANE (*suddenly*). That I never would sir.

She tries to stifle a sob.

I wish I had never been born. I wish I had never come to
Thornfield.

ROCHESTER. Because you are sorry to leave it?

JANE. I grieve to leave Thornfield. I have lived in it a full, a
delightful life. I have not been excluded from all that is bright
and energetic and high. I have talked face to face with an
original, an expanded mind. I have known you Mr Rochester
and now I must be torn from you forever.

ROCHESTER. Why Jane?

JANE. Why? Have you not just told me you will shortly be married, to one inferior to you, to one I do not believe you truly love?

JANE *walks away.*

ROCHESTER. Don't go.

JANE *turns.* BERTHA *is frantic. Flinging herself against the door.*

JANE (*with violence*). Don't go? Do you think I can stay to become nothing to you? Do you think I am an automaton, a machine without feelings? Do you think because I am poor, obscure and plain that I am soul-less and heartless? You are wrong. I have as much soul as you and full as much heart. If God had given me beauty and wealth I should make it as hard for you to leave me as it is for me to leave you.

ROCHESTER. Jane. It *is* so.

He takes her in his arms and kisses her passionately.

JANE. It is not so. You are soon to be married. Let me go.

ROCHESTER. Jane, be still. Don't struggle so.

JANE. I will not be still. I have spoken my mind and can go anywhere now. I am a free human being with an independent will which I exert to leave you.

She pushes herself free. He falls to his knees.

ROCHESTER. And your will shall decide your destiny. I offer you my heart. My hand and a share of all my possessions.

JANE. You play a farce.

ROCHESTER. I ask you to pass through life at my side. To be my second self. My earthly companion.

JANE. You have chosen your bride. Don't mock me.

ROCHESTER. My bride is here because my equal is here. Jane, will you marry me?

JANE *stares at him, stunned.*

Do you doubt me?

JANE. Entirely.

ROCHESTER. You have no faith.

JANE. Not a whit.

ROCHESTER. What love have I for Miss Ingram? What love has she for me?

JANE. But . . .

ROCHESTER. I brought her here to sting your jealousy. To make you want me just as I wanted you. You were so secret, so proud, so restrained. Oh, you, you strange, you unearthly thing. I love you as my own flesh. You. Poor, obscure and plain as you are, accept me as a husband.

JANE. What me?

ROCHESTER. You Jane. Will you be mine. Say yes, quickly.

Pause. She studies him.

JANE. Let me look at your face. Turn to the moonlight.

He does so. She looks long and hard at his features.

ROCHESTER. Oh, Jane. You torture me.

JANE. Do you sincerely wish for me to be your wife?

ROCHESTER. I do.

JANE. Then sir I will marry you.

They kiss, the attic door bursts open and BERTHA *runs from the room, stripping off her clothes, throwing them to the floor. She runs and runs, finally falling to the ground at* JANE's *feet, panting and happy.*

Interval.

Scene 25

The following morning. As before JANE *stands with* BERTHA *at her feet in a state of bliss.* BERTHA's *clothes are strewn about the stage as she left them.* GRACE *gathers them up and takes hold of* BERTHA *during the scene.* MRS FAIRFAX *enters looking perplexed. She stares in bewilderment at* JANE.

MRS FAIRFAX. I feel so astonished I hardly know what to say to you. Tell me. Is it actually true that Mr Rochester has asked you to marry him? Don't laugh at me but I really thought he came in there five minutes ago and said that in a month you would be his wife.

JANE (*smiling*). He has said the same thing to me.

MRS FAIRFAX. He has? Do you believe him. Have you accepted him?

JANE. Yes.

MRS FAIRFAX. I could never have thought it. He means to marry you?

JANE. He tells me so.

MRS FAIRFAX (*shakes her head bewildered*). I have never heard of such a thing. He is a gentleman. You are a servant. I am sorry to grieve you but you are so young and have so little experience of men. I wish to put you on your guard. All that glitters is not gold. Can it really be for love he wants to marry you?

BERTHA *tries to wrestle free.* GRACE *holds fast.*

JANE (*bursting out*). Why not? Am I a monster? Is it impossible that Mr Rochester should have sincere affection for me?

BERTHA *is dragged up the stairs to the attic.*

MRS FAIRFAX. Believe me, you cannot be too careful. Try and keep Mr Rochester at a distance. Distrust yourself as well as him. Gentlemen in his station are not accustomed to marry their governesses.

MR ROCHESTER *appears.*

ROCHESTER. Is that so? This morning I wrote to my bankers in London to send me certain jewels he has in his keeping. Heirlooms of the ladies of Thornfield. In a day or two I shall pour them into your lap. Every attention, every privilege that I would accord a peer's daughter shall be yours. You may go Mrs Fairfax.

She leaves. JANE *is panic-stricken. In the attic* GRACE *forces* BERTHA *back into her clothes.*

JANE. Never mind jewels. Jewels for Jane Eyre sounds unnatural.

ROCHESTER. I will put the diamond chain around your neck.

He kisses her neck.

I will clasp the bracelets on these fine wrists and load these fairy-like fingers with rings.

He caresses her arms and takes her hand to kiss it. She snatches it away.

JANE. No. No, sir. Don't address me as if I were a beauty. I am your plain quakerish governess.

ROCHESTER. I will dress my bride in satin and lace. I will cover the head I love best in a priceless veil and . . .

JANE. And then you won't know me sir and I shall not be your Jane Eyre any longer.

ROCHESTER. You will be my angel.

JANE. I will be myself Mr Rochester. You must not expect anything celestial of me for you will not get it, any more than I shall expect it of you.

ROCHESTER. What do you expect of me Janet. Tell me.

JANE. For a little while, a week or two you will perhaps be as you are now. Then you will begin to find fault with me. You will see that I am not as you thought. That I am far from being an angel, very far. I am capable of things you cannot now imagine.

BERTHA *cries out as* GRACE *binds her wrists.*

ROCHESTER. How strangely you talk, you mysterious creature.

JANE. Then you shall become distant and cool and nothing I do will please you. You laugh at me but I wonder how you will answer a year from now, should I ask for something it does not suit you to give?

ROCHESTER. Ask me something now Jane. The least thing.
I desire to be entreated.

JANE. I ask only this. Don't send for jewels. Don't buy satin
or lace. I could never bear to be dressed like a doll nor could
I act the part. I shall continue as Adele's governess. By that
I shall earn my board and lodging and thirty pounds a year
besides. I shall furnish my own wardrobe and you shall give
me nothing but . . .

ROCHESTER. But what?

JANE. Your regard. And if I give you mine in return that will be
quits.

ROCHESTER. Very well.

He goes to kiss her but she turns away.

She tries to leave.

ROCHESTER. Will you dine with me tonight?

JANE. No thank you sir. I have never dined with you and see no
reason why I should now until . . .

ROCHESTER. Until what?

JANE. Until . . . I can't help it.

ROCHESTER. Until we are married.

JANE. You may send for me as usual at seven o'clock if you wish.

She curtsies and leaves.

Scene 26

JANE'*s bedroom. The eve of the wedding.* MRS FAIRFAX *is
packing a final trunk.* ADELE *is parading around the room
holding* JANE'*s veil to her head.* JANE *looks on uneasily.*

MRS FAIRFAX. Adele, take it off. It's trailing in the . . .

ADELE. Oh, please say you'll let me hold your train. I have never
heard of a wedding before without a bridesmaid.

MRS FAIRFAX (*sternly*). Adele!

ADELE *continues to fondle the material lovingly.*

MRS FAIRFAX. Come and help me tie on the labels.

JANE. Not yet.

MRS FAIRFAX. You would be sorry to lose your luggage and for no-one to know who it belonged to or where it was going.

ADELE. And such a wonderful destination. Maman used to say that Venice was the most romantic city in the whole of the . . .

JANE. Not yet. In the morning.

MRS FAIRFAX. But there is so much to do in the morning. We must dress you and do your hair and . . .

JANE (*sharply*). As I have said my hair will do just as always and it never took me longer than five minutes to dress.

ADELE *and* MRS FAIRFAX *exchange a look.*

ADELE (*showing* JANE *the veil*). It is so beautiful. The roses. I can almost smell them they look so real. You see, there are pearls for dew drops. Mr Rochester must have spent a fortune.

JANE (*suddenly*). Thank you. Thank you. You may leave me now.

ADELE *drapes the veil around* JANE's *shoulders.* MRS FAIRFAX *and* ADELE *leave.*

JANE *stands with the veil in her hands not knowing what to do. She holds it up to the light and sees the exquisite stitching. For a moment she drapes it from her head. She takes a step, watching it billow behind her. Suddenly panicked she screws the veil up and lies down to sleep.* JANE *heaves in her sleep. She is sleep-talking. Arguing with* ROCHESTER *about wearing the veil. Again the words should not be audible.*

JANE. I cannot . . . No . . . I will not . . . You promised . . . Yes. Yes.

Her heavings suggest both the longing and fear she feels at the prospect of her marriage. She wrestles with the veil.

BERTHA *enters the room. She has her wrists tied so that her arms are bound across her chest as in a straight jacket. She is searching for something which she cannot find.* JANE *shifts, becoming more agitated.* BERTHA *sees the veil, the object of her search. She teases the veil from* JANE's *grasp.* JANE *cries out.* JANE *begins to unbutton her top and skirt.* BERTHA *tries to put the veil on. It is a difficult operation with her bound wrists. She tries to look at her reflection in the hand mirror, then, dropping it, she wrenches the veil from her head and using her teeth and foot, rips it in two. The ripping of the veil calls* JANE *from sleep. She wakes to see the torn veil lying on the ground.*

Scene 27

The morning of the wedding. MR ROCHESTER *walks to and fro anxiously as a servant carries luggage through to the carriage.* ADELE *runs to and fro excited.*

ROCHESTER. Is the carriage ready?

FOOTMAN. Yes, sir.

ROCHESTER. And the luggage?

FOOTMAN. We're bringing it right now sir.

The FOOTMAN *exits with an armful of luggage.* ADELE *reads the label on* JANE's *case with relish.*

ADELE. Mrs Rochester. The Grand Hotel. Venice. Italy.

The FOOTMAN *returns for the final case.*

ROCHESTER. Be sure it is outside the church and ready to go the moment we are through. You understand?

FOOTMAN. Yes, sir.

JANE *enters wearing her wedding dress. The veil is nowhere to be seen.* MRS FAIRFAX *follows her in a fluster.*

MRS FAIRFAX. You say you have looked everywhere? I cannot think what could have . . .

JANE. Don't worry. I am as happy without. At least I will be able to see where I'm going. Wish me luck.

MRS FAIRFAX *kisses her.* JANE *goes to leave.*

MRS FAIRFAX. Stop. Look at yourself in the mirror.

JANE *does so. It is a strange sight.*

JANE. Who is it? It seems like a stranger. Come and stand beside me so that I can see something I recognise and make it real.

MRS FAIRFAX *comes to her side.*

MRS FAIRFAX. You are sure you cannot find . . .

JANE. Thank you. I am ready.

They embrace.

The sound of bells as ROCHESTER *and* JANE *walk down the aisle.*

During the following scene BERTHA *becomes increasingly agitated. She responds particularly to the mention of her name.*

Scene 28

CLERGYMAN. Therefore if any man can show any just cause why they may not be lawfully joined together, let him speak now, or else hereafter forever hold his peace. (*Pause. He addresses the bride and bridegroom.*) I require and charge ye both as ye will answer at the day of judgement when the secrets of all hearts shall be disclosed that if either of you know any impediment why ye may not be lawfully joined in matrimony, ye do now confess it, for be you well assured that so many as are coupled together otherwise than God's word doth allow are not joined together by . . .

MASON. The marriage cannot go on. I declare an impediment.

There is a horrible silence.

ROCHESTER (*to the* CLERGYMAN). Proceed.

CLERGYMAN. I cannot.

MASON. I can prove my allegation.

CLERGYMAN. What is its nature? Perhaps it may be got over.

MASON. Hardly. Mr Rochester has a wife already. I affirm and can prove that on the thirteenth of October eighteen thirty-four Edward Rochester married my sister Bertha Mason in Spanish Town Jamaica. It is written here in the record of their marriage.

CLERGYMAN. And is she still living?

MASON. She was living three months ago. She is living at Thornfield Hall. I saw her there.

CLERGYMAN. That cannot be so. I live close by and never heard of or saw such a person.

ROCHESTER. Enough. Enough. (*To the* CLERGYMAN.) What this man says is true. I have been married and the woman to

whom I was married lives. You say you have never heard of a
Mrs Rochester but I dare say you have heard gossip about the
mysterious lunatic kept at Thornfield under lock and guard.
Some have said she is my bastard half-sister, some say my
cast-off mistress, is that not so? I inform you now that she is
my wife whom I married fifteen years ago. Bertha Mason is
mad. Just how mad you shall see for yourselves. I invite you to
come up to the house and visit her. You shall judge for yourself
whether or not I had the right to break the contract.

BERTHA *howls. The party leave the church.* ROCHESTER
clasps JANE*'s hand. They hurry towards the house followed
by* MASON *and the* CLERGYMAN.

They climb the stairs to the attic. ROCHESTER *unlocks the
door.* GRACE POOLE *looks on as* BERTHA *scurries to and
fro 'like some strange wild animal', snatching and growling.
She looks at* ROCHESTER *and a pained, confused expression
crosses her face.*

ROCHESTER. Good morning, Mrs Poole. How is your charge
today?

BERTHA *cries out, rearing up.*

GRACE. Ah she sees you sir. You'd better not stay.

ROCHESTER. Only a few moments, Grace. You must allow me a
few moments.

GRACE. Take care then sir.

ROCHESTER. Keep out of the way.

JANE *stares with horror at the creature in front of her,
recognising her instantly as the self that she left long ago
locked in the red room. She looks away and hides her eyes.*
BERTHA *snaps and snarls.*

MASON. We had better leave her.

GRACE. Beware sir.

ROCHESTER *advances towards her. He stretches out his
hand.* BERTHA *whimpers, her eyes filling with tears. She
nuzzles his hand. She reaches out towards him. She tries to
kiss him on the mouth but* ROCHESTER *pushes her away
appalled. Suddenly* BERTHA *springs forward grappling with*
ROCHESTER *as if trying to strangle him.* BERTHA *lays her
teeth into* ROCHESTER*'s shoulder.* ROCHESTER *struggles
with* BERTHA *until finally* GRACE *manages to pull her off.*

ROCHESTER. *That* is my wife. (*He looks to* JANE.) And this
is what I wished to have. This young girl who stands so
grave, so quiet at the gate of hell. Look at the difference.
Compare these dear eyes, this sweet form with that animal.
Then judge me.

JANE *runs from the room.* BERTHA *howls and writhes as*
GRACE *ties her wrists.*

ROCHESTER (*to* MASON *and* CLERGYMAN). Go on. Get out.

JANE *pulls off her wedding dress and then dresses in her old
grey frock.* BERTHA, *now alone and still fettered is
whimpering and whining. A wave of grief sweeps through*
JANE. *Steeling herself,* JANE *goes to leave her room but*
ROCHESTER *is sitting, waiting outside, his head in his hands.
He jumps to his feet. She stares at him.*

ROCHESTER. Well Jane. Not a word of reproach?

Silence.

You know I am a scoundrel.

JANE. Yes, sir.

ROCHESTER. Then tell me so.

JANE. I cannot. I am tired and sick.

She faints. He rushes to her. He takes her in his arms.

He tries to caress and kiss her. She pulls away violently.

ROCHESTER. What is this? You don't love me, is it so? It was
only my station and the rank of wife you valued. Now that you
think me disqualified to be your husband you shrink from me
as if I were a toad or an ape.

JANE. I care nothing for your title. I do love you in spite of
everything. But I must not show it and this is the last time I
must express it.

ROCHESTER. I see. You intend to make yourself a stranger. To
live under this roof as Adele's governess while to me you will
be cold and distant.

JANE. No, sir. Adele must have a new governess.

ROCHESTER. You are right. She shall be sent to school and you
must endure only one more night under this roof and we will
away. I have a house in France, a remote idyllic spot. There

you will live a happy life free from falsehood and slander. There you will become my wife.

JANE. No, sir. I must leave you.

ROCHESTER. Leave me? What is it you want? I shall fetch it for you. Only speak.

JANE. I must leave Thornfield.

ROCHESTER. Of course. I told you we must go as soon as . . .

JANE. I must part from you for the whole of my life and never see you again.

ROCHESTER. No Jane. It cannot be.

JANE. It cannot be otherwise. (*She gets up to leave.*)

ROCHESTER. You consider me accounted for, is that it? You consider me married? It was my father who contrived for us to marry. She possessed a great fortune and he was a grasping avaricious man. I arrived in Spanish Town, a young man full of the excitement of six weeks on the open seas. I fell instantly in love with that tropical clime where the light is golden and the air warm. Oranges grow on the trees Jane. There are flowers that open at night and blaze like fires. It was as if I had arrived in Paradise. She was then just seventeen and a great beauty.

BERTHA *as she was then comes dancing into the room.*

She was shown to me at parties, splendidly dressed.

A group of men surround her, ROCHESTER *among them. They admire and applaud.*

She would dance and sing. She was an exquisite creature, raised to enchant, to seduce. All the men seemed to admire her and envy me.

She dances into ROCHESTER*'s arms. He sweeps her up into the air. She laughs.*

I was dazzled, stimulated, excited, and being young and ignorant, I thought I loved her. A marriage took place before I knew it.

They kiss. The crowd throw confetti. She laughs and continues to dance. She begins to flirt with other men.

It was not long before I discovered her true nature. She loved to dance and every night insisted that we go to some lavish

entertainment. When I opposed her she became violent and
abusive.

The dance is becoming wilder. He tries to restrain her. She is
furious. He grapples with her, holding her by the wrists. She
pulls free. The dance becomes highly sexual as she teases and
tantalises the men in defiance of ROCHESTER.

She began to drink and would escape the house, running away
for days at a time, returning when she had run out of money,
which never took long. For I soon discovered she had an
appetite for every kind of excess and yes . . . .

She kisses a man, a stranger.

. . . for other men. I lived with that woman for four years at the
end of which the doctors declared her mad. She was shut up in
her bedroom and tended by a nurse. You could hear her curses
day and night, no harlot ever had a fouler vocabulary than she.
I approached the very verge of despair. I was on the point of
suicide.

JANE. How came you then sir to England?

ROCHESTER. It was one night. I had been awakened by her
yells. There had been a thunderstorm so to cool myself I
walked in my wet garden. Amidst the dripping orange trees, the
drenched pineapples, the dawn of the tropics kindled around
me and a voice from Europe whispered in my ear. 'Up' it said,
'Live again. Take the maniac to England. Confine her at
Thornfield then go, travel, form a new tie. That woman who
has so long abused you is not your wife, nor are you her
husband.'

JANE. You speak of her with such hatred, such loathing. It is
cruel. She cannot help being mad.

ROCHESTER. That I knew and would not abandon her as I might
have. I brought her home. I saw that she was cared for and
treated kindly and then I left her. My own presence enraged her
then as it does to this day. I sought my ideal woman in France
in Italy and Spain. I could not find her yet I could not live
alone. I tried the companionship of mistresses but it was a
grovelling existence.

Pause.

So it was that finally I returned to England, corroded with
disappointment, sourly disposed against all womankind. On

a frosty winter afternoon I rode towards Thornfield, abhorred
spot, expecting no peace, no pleasure there. On my way
I passed a figure, a childish and slender creature.

We hear the sound of horses' hooves.

JANE *looks away as if fighting the memory.*

I had no presentiment of what she would mean to me, no
warning that the arbiter of my life stood there in disguise.
I had fallen from my horse. She offered me help. I was proud
and surly but she would not go away. When I leant upon her
frail shoulder (*He does so.* JANE *closes her eyes aching with
the memory.*) a fresh sap stole into my frame. (*She tears
herself away.*)

JANE. Don't talk any more of those days, sir.

ROCHESTER. No Jane. Why dwell on the past when the future is
so much brighter? You see now how the case stands do you
not? After half a lifetime passed in misery and solitude I have
found what I can truly love. I have found you. My sympathy,
my better self, my good angel, my saviour.

Silence.

Why are you silent Jane?

JANE. I must . . .

ROCHESTER. Janet. Accept my pledge of fidelity and give me
yours.

JANE. I must . . .

ROCHESTER. You understand what I want of you. Just this
promise. 'I will be yours, Mr Rochester.'

JANE. I understand but I . . .

ROCHESTER. Say it now. Quickly.

JANE. Mr Rochester, I cannot be yours.

Silence.

ROCHESTER. Jane, do you mean to go one way in the world and
let me go another?

JANE. I do.

ROCHESTER. Jane. (*Kissing her neck.*) Do you mean it now?

JANE. I do.

ROCHESTER (*kissing her hair*). And now?

JANE. I do.

In spite of her intentions she cannot bring herself to pull away. He pulls her to him.

ROCHESTER. You. You exquisite creature. You unearthly thing. My saviour, my angel, my love.

JANE (*violently tearing herself away*). You must not say those words to me. I must not listen to them. The more solitary, the more unloved, the more friendless I am the better. I have sought myself a heaven on earth. I have thought myself an angel. I have been vain, deluded, drunk with desire. I will atone. I will hold to the principles I had when I was sane and not mad as I am now.

Suddenly she runs to him, falling at his feet and kissing his hand wildly. She dare not look into his face. As he comes down to her she pulls away, running from him as fast as she can. She runs and runs until she is exhausted, stumbling forward over the uneven ground. Finally she falls to the earth. She closes her eyes. ROCHESTER appears in her imagination. He takes her hand. She kisses his hand wildly just as she did before leaving him. She flings him off and staggers on.

JANE. No. I will not look back. The past is a page so heavenly, so sweet, so sad. To read one line would . . .

Finally she drops to the ground exhausted and sleeps.

Scene 29

Three days later. JANE awakens to the sound of a busy market. She is very hungry. Someone is selling bread from a basket. Someone else chickens. Another apples. Customers come and go. People cross the square with bundles and bags laden with things. JANE stands and watches, an outsider. When the GIRL selling bread is alone, she goes to her.

JANE. Excuse me. Do you know of any place where a servant is needed or a dressmaker?

GIRL. Not that I've heard of.

JANE. What is the trade in this place? What work do people do?

GIRL. Farm labourers. Or else they work at the needle factory.

JANE. Do they employ women?

GIRL. No.

A man passes selling plums. JANE looks on. She is hungry.

JANE. Would you give me a piece of fruit in exchange for this handkerchief?

MAN. What would I want with your handkerchief?

JANE. Or my gloves. They are recently bought.

The man walks swiftly away calling 'Plums! Fresh plums'. She approaches a passer-by.

JANE. Excuse me, can you tell me if someone might need a servant in the village or where I might . . .

PASSER-BY. There's not much call for servants round here. (*He goes on his way.*)

JANE sees a man enter eating a pie.

JANE. Will you give me a bite of your pie. I am very hungry.

MAN. You should be ashamed of yourself. A lady like you asking for other people's food.

He walks away. A GIRL comes out onto a doorstep and pours milk into a saucer.

GIRL. Here, Kitty, kitty. Here.

As soon as she has gone back inside, JANE picks up the saucer of milk and drinks it. She replaces the bowl and walks away quickly. We hear the sound of distant thunder. People are hurrying for shelter, putting up umbrellas. JANE is left alone. Within moments she is drenched to the skin. The occasional figure hurries across the stage, heading homeward. The sky darkens. There is a lightning flash and a crack of thunder overhead.

JANE. Must I spend yet another night out of doors? Must I sleep again on the cold drenched ground? Oh Lord, I am weak and hungry. Why will I not let myself die? Why do I struggle to retain a useless life?

A pause and then quietly:

Because I know, at least – I hope, that Mr Rochester is living.

He appears behind her as before. He takes her hand. She kisses his hand wildly. As she turns to embrace him he disappears. She drops to her knees.

Forgive me, Lord. I am weak and foolish.

Huge crack of thunder.

All men must die. Oh Lord let me stiffen with the frost. Let me decay and mingle with the earth. Let me know the numbness of death and lose all sensation that I may never again long for what I cannot have.

Thunderclap. Darkness.

Scene 30

The parlour of a cottage. SAINT JOHN RIVERS *carries* JANE *in his arms. His sisters* MARY *and* DIANA *stare at* JANE. SAINT JOHN *puts her down. She is shaking.*

DIANA. Who is it?

MARY. She looks white.

DIANA. She will fall. Let her sit.

　　DIANA *brings her a chair. She sits with help from* MARY.

MARY. She is so thin.

DIANA. Is she ill or only famished? Fetch some bread and milk.

SAINT JOHN (*crouching in front of* JANE). What is your name?

JANE. Jane . . . Elliot.

SAINT JOHN. And where do you live? Where are your friends?

　　Silence.

Can we send for anyone?

　　JANE *shakes her head. They dip the bread into the milk and hold it to her lips.*

MARY. Try. Try to eat.

　　JANE *thrusts her mouth into the bowl desperate for food.*

SAINT JOHN. Not so much. Restrain her. She will choke.

DIANA. Take off her wet clothes.

> DIANA *and* MARY *do so, easing her out of the sodden cloth.*

> It is well you took her in Saint John. She would have been found dead in the morning.

MARY. I wonder who she is?

SAINT JOHN. She is not uneducated. Her accent is pure.

MARY. Her clothes though wet and muddy are little worn and of good quality.

DIANA. Let them be cleaned. She will stay here until she is well enough to leave.

Scene 31

An evening several days later. DIANA, MARY *and* SAINT JOHN *sit together reading. There are books scattered on the floor.* JANE *comes slowly towards them. She has come downstairs for the first time.*

DIANA. What good news! Your strength is back.

> *In unison.*

MARY. You should have called for help. Sit down.

DIANA. You must be hungry.

SAINT JOHN. It is well her fever has subdued her appetite. It would be dangerous to give in to craving. She may eat but only a little.

JANE. I trust I shall not eat long at your expense.

SAINT JOHN. As soon as you tell us where you have come from you may be restored.

> *Pause .*

JANE. That I cannot do. I am absolutely without home or friends.

> *All three stop and look at* JANE, *puzzling her story.*

SAINT JOHN. Where did you last reside?

MARY (*quietly*). Saint John let her be. We can question her later.

JANE. The name of the place and of the person with whom I lived must be a secret. I fear discovery above all else.

SAINT JOHN. But if I know nothing I cannot help you and it is help that you need is it not?

JANE. I need to find a job and thereby means to keep myself.

SAINT JOHN. I see.

JANE. Show me how to work or how to seek work. That is all I ask.

SAINT JOHN. I shall endeavour to find you employment. I have no great powers you understand. I am a village clergyman. My aid will be of the humblest sort

JANE. I will take whatever may be found.

SAINT JOHN (*looks at his watch*). I must out again. There is a baby born at the heights.

MARY. But Saint John, it is so far.

DIANA. Can it not wait till morning? Surely the baby will not know the difference.

MARY. And look, it is starting to rain.

SAINT JOHN. If I let a gust of wind or a sprinkling of rain turn me aside from these easy tasks, what preparation would it be for the life I'll soon lead.

A silence falls. The sisters catch each other's eyes. He leaves.

JANE. Is he going away?

DIANA. He plans to go to India to work as a missionary.

JANE. He's a brave man.

MARY. Too brave I fear.

The two sisters stand looking out of the window as SAINT JOHN *disappears into the darkness.* JANE *has picked up a book.*

JANE (*shyly*). Someone is studying Italian?

DIANA. Oh yes. Do you read it?

JANE. A little.

DIANA. Such a beautiful language. It sounds like a song. Don't you think?

JANE. I have never heard it spoken.

DIANA. Then you will hear it tonight after supper.

Scene 32

Some weeks later. MARY, DIANA *and* JANE *are sitting together in the parlour. There is a fond, easy atmosphere between them.* DIANA *reads aloud a poem.* SAINT JOHN *enters the room.*

DIANA. The sun descending in the west. The evening star does shine. The birds are silent in their nests . . .

SAINT JOHN (*clears his throat. They stand*). I have some news for you with regard to future employment Jane. I would have told you some weeks back but I saw how my sisters enjoyed your company and . . .

DIANA. You have found her something Saint John? That's wonderful.

SAINT JOHN. You need be in no hurry to hear. You may even think it degrading. I see now your habits have been what the world calls refined. Your society has been amongst the educated, but I consider that no service degrades which can better our race. I hold that the more arid, the more unreclaimed the soil, the scantier mead our toil brings, the higher the honour.

We can hear SAINT JOHN *the preacher speaking.*

Pause .

JANE. Well what is it to be?

Pause.

DIANA. Tell us, Saint John. We are waiting.

SAINT JOHN. Two years ago when I came to this parish there was no school. The children of the poor were excluded from every hope of progress. I first established a school for boys and mean now to open a second for girls. I am asking you to become the teacher of twenty or so pupils. They will be poor farmers' daughters. Knitting, sewing, reading and writing will be all that is required. What you will do with your accomplishments, with your mind and aspirations I do not know. For certain they will not be needed in such a place.

JANE. They will save till they are wanted. They will keep.

SAINT JOHN. You know then what you undertake and are prepared to do it?

JANE. I thank you for your proposal Mr Rivers and accept it with all my heart. I hope that one day I may repay your kindness.

Scene 33

The schoolroom. JANE sits amidst a class of GIRLS. She is teaching a geography lesson and has a globe in front of her.

JANE (*pointing to the letters on the globe*). America. Say it together.

CLASS. America.

JANE. And who can tell me the name of this set of islands here? It is written on the globe. See if you can read it.

CHILD 1. The W . . . est . . . Indians.

JANE. Indies. The West Indies.

CHILD 2. Is it a very long way off, Miss?

JANE. Thousands of miles. It would take weeks to sail there in a boat.

CHILD 3. How many weeks, Miss?

JANE. Six . . . I believe. Or thereabouts.

CHILD 1. What is it like?

JANE. I am told . . . or at least I have read that it is very beautiful. A paradise almost, where the light is golden and the air is warm, and oranges grow on the . . .

ROCHESTER *appears behind her. Bends down and kisses her neck. She stands up, flustered and turns her back on the class and stares off.*

CHILD 3. On the trees, Miss?

JANE. Yes. Yes. On the trees.

CHILD 1. What else, Miss?

JANE. What else?

CHILD 1. Apart from oranges?

JANE (*she turns back to face the class*). It is green. Very green. Because of the rainfall. There are tropical storms . . . and hurricanes. Hurricanes that uproot trees and smash whole houses.

CHILD 2. What is a hurricane, Miss?

JANE. A hurricane.

ROCHESTER *lifts her in his arms and twirls her through the air. The children do not see* ROCHESTER *or the dance as it takes place in* JANE's *imagination.*

It is a strong wind that nothing can stop, that tears in a great circle and carries everything with it and . . .

She sits back down. ROCHESTER *disappears.*

CHILD 1. Yes, Miss?

JANE (*she gathers herself*). Thank you. Thank you. That is all for today.

The class disperses. When JANE *is alone she puts her hand to her mouth and lets out a sob. At that moment* SAINT JOHN *appears. She quickly dries her eyes and sets about clearing up after the lesson.*

SAINT JOHN. Have you found your first week harder than you expected?

JANE. No. On the contrary.

SAINT JOHN. Perhaps your accommodation – your cottage has disappointed you?

JANE. Not at all. I am grateful for all you have done.

SAINT JOHN. In that case I shall make my request. I have decided to teach myself Hindustani in view of my imminent departure to India. I need . . . that is, it would be of great assistance to me if you were to join me in the task and become my pupil. In teaching you I shall sharpen my own understanding.

Pause.

JANE. I . . .

SAINT JOHN. Lessons will be held every day for two hours here in the schoolroom before class. I trust that will suit. I leave in less than six months so you will not have to make the sacrifice for long.

Pause.

JANE. Very well.

SAINT JOHN. You are in agreement. Excellent. We shall begin tomorrow. Tomorrow at six. Good day.

She watches him go, puzzled.

Scene 34

Some weeks later. JANE and JOHN are finishing their morning's lesson.

SAINT JOHN. Very good. (*Looks at his watch.*) Very good.

JANE. I begin to regret that I will never have cause to use it.

He closes the textbook .

SAINT JOHN. Indeed?

JANE. After such labours, I mean.

SAINT JOHN. Well Jane. That is a subject on which I wish to speak to you.

She looks at him with a sudden premonition of what is coming.

You know that it is now only two weeks before I leave.

JANE. May God protect you.

SAINT JOHN. Yes. There is my joy, my glory. I go as God's servant. I have been called to rise, to spread my wings, to use my powers to do that which is sacred. A year ago Jane I can tell you now, I feared I had made a mistake in entering the clergy. I burned for more stimulation. I fancied myself an author, an orator, an artist. Anything but a priest in a country parish. But then after a season of darkness the light came into my life.

JANE. I am glad for you. (*She busies herself with tidying books.*).

SAINT JOHN. Since that moment I have lived as one blessed.
Imagine Jane the joy of knowing you are chosen to undertake
the Lord's greatest task. To sacrifice every inclination, every
pleasure to a greater cause. To leave behind a life of selfish ease
and barren obscurity and become the Lord's own messenger.
It seems strange to me that all do not burn to do the same.

JANE. All have not your powers Saint John. It would be folly for
the weak to march with the strong.

SAINT JOHN. I do not speak to the feeble Jane. I speak to one
who has great strength and faith.

BERTHA *appears in her attic, bound and gagged and tied to
her chair.*

JANE. Forgive me but it is after eight and I must . . .

SAINT JOHN. Come with me, Jane.

JANE. Oh, Saint John. Have mercy.

SAINT JOHN. God and nature intended you for a missionary's
wife. I claim you, not for my pleasure but for the Lord's own
army.

JANE. I am not fit for it. I have no vocation.

SAINT JOHN. But who is fit for such a task? And is not humility
the ground on which all Christian virtue must grow?

JANE. Nothing speaks or stirs in me when you talk. No light
enters my soul. I feel only dread.

SAINT JOHN. I have watched you since first you came and am
certain now that you were sent for a purpose. You are hard-
working and conscientious in all that you do. I see a soul that
revels in the flame and excitement of sacrifice. You have
precisely the qualities that the task requires. And if, as it seems,
there is something in your past you wish to escape or forget,
what better means than to devote yourself to God and humanity

JANE. A moment. Let me think.

Pause. BERTHA *writhes and struggles.* JANE *wrestles with
her conscience. She is extremely agitated.*

I understand what you say. And you are right that in staying
here I nurture a hope that were better forgot. It is true that it
would be an honour to be thus chosen and I have often longed
to see the world.

Pause.

SAINT JOHN. Do you agree?

JANE. I agree to go to India. But not as your wife.

SAINT JOHN. Our union must be consecrated or it cannot exist.

JANE. I cannot marry you.

SAINT JOHN. Why this refusal?

JANE. Because you do not love me. Let me be your fellow-missionary and speak no more of marriage.

SAINT JOHN. How can I, a man not yet thirty take to India a girl of nineteen unless she is my wife. (*He clears his throat.*) Doubtless, enough love would follow upon marriage to make it right even in your eyes.

BERTHA *has untied herself from the chair. She flings herself against the door.*

JANE (*violently*). I scorn your idea of love. And I scorn you when you offer it.

SAINT JOHN (*shocked*). You surprise me, Jane. I had not expected such vehemence from you. I shall leave you now. There are yet two weeks for you to consider my proposal. Remember if you reject me it is not me you deny but God.

He goes. She prays. She is in torment. BERTHA *bites at the rope on her wrists.*

JANE. Oh Lord. He is a good, a brave, a virtuous man. He saved my life and gave me means to live. I know these things and yet I shudder at the thought of a union. He does not love me, though he would no doubt observe love's customs. Every endearment, every touch would be a sacrifice made on principle. Any response unwanted. For I fear, were I forced to marry I would develop a strange tortured love for him. He is so heroic, so talented, so sure. But he. He would not want my love. I would be always restrained, forced to keep the fire of my nature hidden, to strangle all that is alive and . . .

(*She stops herself.*) Forgive me Lord. Teach me.

Tell me. Am I sent to be his wife?

BERTHA*'s hands are free. She lights the flaming torch. She opens the door of the attic and descends the stairs. She has become the fire.*

Scene 35

MARY, DIANA, JANE *and* SAINT JOHN *are at table. He is mid-sermon.*

SAINT JOHN. He will wipe away every tear from their eyes. There will be no more death or mourning or crying or pain for the old order of things has passed away. There will be no more night. They will not need the light of a lamp or the light of the sun for the Lord will give them light. To he who is thirsty he will give drink from the spring of the water of life. He who overcomes will inherit all. The cowardly, the fearful and the unbelieving, their place will be in the fiery lake of burning sulphur. They will be tormented day and night forever and ever.

BERTHA *lets out a wild cry. People run in all directions shouting. Thornfield is on fire. In the middle of it all we see* BERTHA *climbing to the battlements carrying a flame. She stands on the roof of the burning Thornfield.* ROCHESTER *begins to climb to her rescue.*

Meanwhile SAINT JOHN *and* JANE *are alone.*

SAINT JOHN. If I listened to my pride I would say no more to you of marriage but I listen to my duty. To the word of God who claims you for his own. (*He lays his hand on her forehead.*) Jane repent, resolve while there is yet time.

JANE (*slowly*). I could marry you if I were certain, were I convinced that it is God's will. I *could* vow to marry you here and now.

SAINT JOHN. My prayers are answered.

JANE. Oh Lord. Show me. Show me the path.

ROCHESTER *has reached the roof. He takes hold of* BERTHA, *holding her in his arms as if he were a human strait jacket. It is a strange contortion – half embrace, half bondage.*

BERTHA (*cries out*). Jane! Jane! Jane!

JANE *hears her cry. She looks wildly about her.*

SAINT JOHN. What is it?

BERTHA *and* ROCHESTER. Jane! Jane!

JANE (*looking up to the heavens she cries out*). I am coming! Wait for me!

Scene 36

JANE *stands in her shawl and bonnet. She stares at the wreckage of the fire, now deserted. She picks her way through the debris as if looking for some clue, some sign of life. We recognise the furniture of Thornfield, smashed and charred. We hear the sound of rooks cawing and the moaning of the wind.* BERTHA *is sitting waiting in the attic. The door hangs open. She is peaceful now as if the rage she felt as a prisoner has left her. From this point onwards* BERTHA *is present as she was at the beginning.* JANE *climbs the great staircase and enters the attic. She stares at the charred remains of the room. She sits down slowly in the chair on* BERTHA's *lap.* BERTHA *touches her gently. In returning to Thornfield and following her true desires* JANE *can reunite with her secret self.*

A WOMAN *scavenges in the debris. She is blackened like the ruined house, and has a leering, threatening presence.*

JANE. Excuse me.

JANE *runs down the stairs.* BERTHA *follows very slowly.*

Can you tell me, do you know Mr Rochester who was once master of this house?

WOMAN. Indeed. I was once the late master's parlour maid.

JANE. The late! Is he dead?

WOMAN. No, no. That was some twenty years back. His son is now the master . . . or was until the fire.

JANE. How did it happen?

WOMAN. There was a lady kept in the house, confined to the attic . . .

JANE. I have heard something of it.

WOMAN. They say she was a lunatic. For years even them living in the house didn't know she was there. But a strange thing happened a year since. A very strange thing. There was a young lady, a governess at the hall . . .

JANE. How was the fire started?

WOMAN. . . . that Mr Rochester fell in love with . . .

JANE. When did it happen?

WOMAN. The servants say they never saw anyone so much in love as he was. She was a little insignificant thing and half his age. But he was bewitched they say, and decided to marry her.

JANE. Did the lunatic – the woman in the attic – start the fire?

WOMAN. Exactly so. The lunatic, so it turned out was none other than Mr Rochester's lawful wedded wife. When this was discovered the young governess ran away. Mr Rochester sought her as if she had been the most precious thing in the world. But he never found her. He grew terrible wild in his disappoint-ment. He became quite a hermit and desolate with it. They say that he would sit outside the attic door rocking like baby for he was now as mad as she. He'd talk through the locked door. Strange broken sentences full of regret. It was he who tried to rescue her on the night of the fire. She had climbed from the attic window up onto the roof. I witnessed the struggle he had to get to her. But when, at last, he held her in his arms she sprang forward. The next minute she lay smashed to pieces.

Pause.

JANE. Dead?

WOMAN. Aye.

JANE. And were there other lives lost?

WOMAN. No. Perhaps it would have been better if there had been.

JANE. What do you mean?

MAN. Poor Mr Rochester. Some say it was a judgement on him for keeping his marriage secret.

JANE. You said he was alive.

WOMAN. Alive, yes. But some think he would be better dead.

JANE. Why? How? Where is he?

WOMAN. He is stone blind.

JANE. Blind?

BERTHA *lays her hand gently on* JANE's *forehead.*

WOMAN. He was taken from under the ruins alive but badly hurt. One hand was crushed and his eyesight gone.

JANE. Where is he? Where does he live now?

WOMAN. At Ferndean. A farmhouse he has deep in the forest some thirty miles off. It is a desolate spot.

JANE. Have you a horse and cart?

WOMAN. Aye.

JANE. I need to go there. Today. This instant. As soon as I may. I will pay you a week's wages.

BERTHA *pulls* JANE *in a circle, urging her on towards Ferndean.*

Scene 37

JANE *and* BERTHA *approach Ferndean. It is a misty evening. She stops suddenly as she sees through the gloom, a figure,* MR ROCHESTER, *now blind. His hair is overgrown and right hand cradled out of view. He reminds* JANE *of 'some wronged and fettered wild beast or bird, dangerous to approach in his sullen woe'.* MRS FAIRFAX *comes out of the house.*

MRS FAIRFAX. Will you take my arm sir? There's a downpour coming on. Sir, you'll be soaked through.

ROCHESTER *shakes his head.*

ROCHESTER. Leave me be.

ROCHESTER *walks forward a few paces towards* JANE. *He stops only inches from her. He stretches out his hand, almost but not quite touching her, to feel the light evening rain.* BERTHA *and* JANE *reach out towards him. He turns away and returns to the house.*

Scene 38

MRS FAIRFAX *is sitting over a bowl peeling apples.* JANE *and* BERTHA *appear behind her. There is a moment before* MRS FAIRFAX *realises there is anybody there. When she does she starts up dropping the bowl and fruit. She stares at* JANE.

MRS FAIRFAX. Is it really you?

JANE *stretches out her hand which* MRS FAIRFAX *takes and presses to her cheek.*

MRS FAIRFAX. Oh my girl. My girl.

A hand bell rings.

JANE. Tell your master that a person wishes to speak to him but do not give him my name.

MRS FAIRFAX. He'll not see you. He refuses everyone.

She hurries away. JANE takes in the small kitchen. MRS FAIRFAX returns.

MRS FAIRFAX. You are to send in your name and your business.

She fills a glass with water from a jug.

JANE. Is that what he sent for? Here. Let me take it.

JANE and BERTHA enters the parlour. PILOT leaps up from beside his master and bounds towards her, excited. She strokes his head to quieten him. BERTHA leads him away to a corner. She watches the scene. JANE hands ROCHESTER the water and he drinks it.

ROCHESTER. Thank you Mrs Fairfax.

JANE. Mrs Fairfax is in the kitchen.

ROCHESTER. Who is this?

He reaches out but does not touch her.

Answer me. Speak again.

JANE. Will you have a little more water sir? I have spilt half the glass.

ROCHESTER. Jane.

JANE. Yes, sir.

ROCHESTER. What delusion. What sweet madness is this?

JANE. No delusion. No madness. It is I sir.

ROCHESTER (*reaching out wildly*). Whatever. Whoever you are. Let me touch you or I cannot live.

She gives him her hand.

Her very fingers. Her wrist. Her arm.

He takes hold of her bit by bit and pulls her to him.

ROCHESTER. It is you is it Jane?

JANE. I came back to you sir.

ROCHESTER. You are not dead in some ditch or under some stream?

JANE. I am here.

ROCHESTER. You are here. And will you stay with me?

JANE. I will.

ROCHESTER. And never leave me?

JANE. Never.

ROCHESTER. Oh sweet angel.

JANE. I will be your eyes and your hands. I will be your nurse, your housekeeper, your companion.

ROCHESTER. But Jane . . .

JANE. Yes, sir?

Pause.

ROCHESTER. I want a wife.

JANE. Then you must ask for one.

ROCHESTER. But you are young. I am old and sightless. A poor blind man you must lead about by the hand.

JANE. Sssh.

ROCHESTER. Jane. Am I not hideous to you?

JANE. Very sir. You always were you know.

ROCHESTER (*smiling in spite of himself*). The wickedness has not been taken out of you then?

JANE. To tell the truth, I love you better. Now that you are not so proud and independent. Now that you are not always the giver and protector.

ROCHESTER. Jane. Give me your hand.

She does so.

Until now I have hated to be helped, to be led, to feel my own weakness. But I shall hate it no more.

Pause.

The door is open into the garden is it not?

They go out into the garden. They stand amidst the fallen apples. BERTHA *moves towards them.*

Tell me. What can you see?

JANE. The rain is over and gone. There is a tender shining after it. The leaves are still wet and dripping but they glitter in the sun.

ROCHESTER *kisses* JANE's *hand.* BERTHA *pulls his hand towards her face, guiding his fingers over her hair, cheeks, eyes, mouth and neck.* ROCHESTER *and* JANE *kiss.*